The INDONESIAN ECONOMY in CRISIS

The INDONESIAN ECONOMY in CRISIS

Causes, Consequences and Lessons

HAL HILL

ST. MARTIN'S PRESS
New York

Published by
Institute of Southeast Asian Studies
30 Heng Mui Keng Terrace
Pasir Panjang Road
Singapore 119614
Internet e-mail: publish@iseas.edu.sg
World Wide Web: http://www.iseas.edu.sg/pub.html

First published in the United States of America in 1999 by
St Martin's Press
Scholarly and Reference Division
175 Fifth Avenue
New York, N.Y. 10010

Library of Congress Cataloguing-in-Publication Data

Hill, Hal, 1948–
   The Indonesian economy in crisis: causes, consequences and
lessons / Hal Hill.
      p.   cm.
Includes bibliographical references and index.
ISBN 0-312-22883-X
   1. Indonesia—Economic policy.   2. Indonesia—Economic
conditions—1945–   3. Indonesia—Social conditions.   I. Title.
HC447.H548   1999
338.9598—dc21   98-38750
                                                                         CIP

ISBN 981-230-058-9 (softcover, ISEAS, Singapore)

For the USA and Canada, this hardcover edition (ISBN 0-312-22883-X) is published
by St. Martin's Press, New York.

Typeset by Superskill Graphics.
Printed in Singapore by Seng Lee Press Pte Ltd

10 9 8 7 6 5 4 3 2 1

CONTENTS

TABLES

FIGURES

ACKNOWLEDGEMENTS

Many people have kindly assisted with comments, advice, information and encouragement. Three good friends, Heinz Arndt, Sisira Jayasuriya, and Chris Manning, read an earlier version and provided very detailed comments. I am especially grateful to Chris Manning, who has in some respects been a "silent partner" throughout this enterprise (though not so silent on the Law School courts, Coombs tea room and cellar bar!), in the course of also producing his own analysis of the crisis (forthcoming as Manning, 1999).

Others who have helped with ideas and discussions include Ross McLeod, Anwar Nasution, Thee Kian Wie (I'm not so optimistic this time, Bung!), Mohammad Sadli (your daily e-mail messages are indispensable, Pak!), Hadi Soesastro, Chandra Athukorala, Peter McCawley, Colin Johnson, Mari Pangestu, Ross Garnaut, Anggito Abimanyu, Mayling Oey, Peter Gardiner, George Fane, and Jamie Mackie. Chatib Basri, Kelly Bird, Colin Johnson, and Bijit Bora kindly assisted with some data requests.

Seminar participants over the past 18 months in Canberra, Jakarta, Singapore, Auckland, Seoul, Kita Kyushu, Hanoi, Sydney, Brisbane, Adelaide, and Melbourne have helped develop my ideas. I learned much from participating in the highly stimulating Canberra workshop of November 1998 on "Indonesia's Economic Crisis", while the weekly seminar programme at the ANU Division of Economics has been a constant source of intellectual enrichment. I also benefited greatly through interacting with the group of contributors to the Arndt & Hill (1999) edited volume on the crisis in Southeast Asia.

As always, I am very pleased to be associated with Triena Ong and her highly efficient and pleasant publications team at ISEAS.

A first draft of this volume was completed in April 1999, and the revised version a month later, just prior to the holding of Indonesia's first reasonably free and fair election in 44 years. Events there are changing exceptionally quickly, and the outlook remains extremely uncertain. Readers are asked to keep these caveats in mind.

May 1999

I

INTRODUCTION

Since the middle of 1997, we have witnessed momentous and tragic events in Indonesia. Momentous because nobody — from the pre-eminent Washington institutions, to rating agencies and academics — foresaw the events, and we still have only an imperfect understanding of their origins and future course. And tragic because ordinary Indonesians are suffering a great deal, and many have experienced a substantial decline in their living standards. As the 1998 annual World Bank (1998a) assessment of the country soberly observed:

> Indonesia is in deep crisis. A country that achieved decades of rapid growth, stability, and poverty reduction, is now near economic collapse. … No country in recent history, let alone one the size of Indonesia, has ever suffered such a dramatic reversal of fortune.

There is a particular irony in Indonesia's case, for it has been by far the worst affected among the four East Asian 'crisis' economies (i.e., along with Korea, Malaysia, and Thailand), and yet initially there was a general expectation that it would not be as adversely affected as Thailand. "Why Indonesia is not Thailand" was a widely held sentiment over the period June–August 1997.

Just as, until recently, explaining why the East Asian economies grew so fast was a major preoccupation of economists and political scientists, now all of a sudden the big question of our time is to

1

understand how and why economies such as Indonesia dramatically fell off their high-growth trajectories. Why didn't economists foresee the events of 1997–98? How can seemingly robust and vigorous economies fall so far, so swiftly? Do we, in consequence, need to change the way we view the world? Is there anything to salvage of the "East Asian miracle"? Is Southeast Asia about to experience its own version of the "lost decade", analogous to that which afflicted much of Africa and Latin America (and, closer to home, the Philippines) in the 1980s?[1]

Several features and implications of the current crisis stand out:

- East Asia's growth momentum has slowed sharply; even in the best case scenarios, per capita GDP growth may be static in 1999 and perhaps next year. In 1998, for the first time in its 31-year history, the economy of ASEAN contracted, by about 5%.
- Within this generally subdued East Asian economic environment, there are large intra-regional variations, from mild recessions to real disasters. While this analysis focuses on the latter, it is worth remembering that Asia's two most populous nations, China and India, have thus far escaped relatively unscathed.
- Indonesia is obviously by far the worst affected economy in East Asia. Its economic contraction has been about twice as large as the next most affected, Thailand, and it is the only crisis economy to experience serious inflation. Its political turmoil and social tension have also obviously been much deeper than elsewhere.
- There is serious socio-economic hardship in the worst affected economies, and in particular rising underemployment and poverty.
- The dimensions and severity of the crisis were not accurately foreseen by anybody — international financial organizations, governments, academics, ratings agencies.
- In the search for causes, it is conceptually important (though empirically tricky) to distinguish between "triggers" and

"contagion". While Thailand is the main example of the former, Indonesia arguably had a foot in both camps.

- This is not the kind of crisis to which governments and international agencies in East Asia are accustomed. In particular, it was not an old-style economic crisis which had its origins in profligate government spending, runaway inflation and hopelessly unrealistic exchange rates.
- The prospects for a quick return to high economic growth are mixed, a problem compounded by the region's economic interdependence and the absence of a regional "locomotive". Nevertheless, while global economic conditions will strongly affect the pace of recovery, economic reform must start at home. Governments' response to the crisis will have a major bearing on how quickly the economic decline is arrested.
- Prognostications which call for the "end of the East Asian style of development" are mistaken. What is needed is reform, albeit substantial, rather than revolution. Just as the region's economic policy technocrats should not be blamed for the current mess, so too should we avoid a wholesale rejection of the policy ingredients of recent decades.

The purpose of this monograph is to describe and analyse Indonesia's most serious economic crisis, against the general backdrop of economic decline in Southeast Asia. We first look at the events leading up to the crisis (Chapter II), followed by a charting of its course from July 1997 to March 1999 (Chapter III). Chapter IV assesses the socio-economic impacts, while Chapter V attempts to explain the crisis, both at the onset and in its subsequent developments. The final two sections look forward, considering Indonesia's immediate policy challenges to overcome the crisis, and dwelling on some of the key longer-term policy challenges raised by the crisis. Chapters V and VII are more analytical in orientation, and I consider them to be the most important; the other sections are essentially descriptive.

One particular methodological point requires emphasis at the outset. These are not events which are amenable to simple theories or uni-dimensional explanations. There is no one single answer to the question "What went wrong?" To construct a convincing story, one has to cast the net widely, drawing on theory, empirics, country detail, and institutions, and recent history, economics and politics. Analyses which focus just on the economics or the politics inevitably miss much of the account. For, at the peak of the crisis in mid-1998, Indonesia experienced a comprehensive collapse in confidence in its currency, its economy, its institutions, its social fabric, and its political leadership. Setting the parameters wide runs the risk of being methodologically untidy, but a narrow approach perforce introduces even higher risks of omission.

II

PRELUDE TO THE CRISIS

Four features of pre-crisis Indonesia stand out. These centre around the absence of any "early warning" indicators of impending collapse,[2] and they set the stage for our subsequent analysis.

First, economic growth was strong, and all available evidence suggested that the benefits continued to be broad-based. The country's statistical agency, BPS, estimated that the percentage of the population in poverty continued to decline in the 1990s, from 15.1% in 1990 to 13.7% in 1993 and 11.3% in 1996. A declining incidence of poverty was found over this period in all 27 provinces, for both rural and urban areas. Inter-personal inequality remained low, and the gini ratios showed no upward trend. Real wages were growing in every sector for which good quality data were available (Manning 1998). Other social indicators, such as educational enrolments, nutritional intake and various indicators of health status, also continued to improve over the decade prior to the crisis. International comparisons (e.g., World Bank 1998*b*, p. 75) confirmed these good results, while also underlining the conclusion that, by East Asian standards, some of Indonesia's social indicators continued to lag somewhat.[3]

It is easy to quibble with these social indicators. Indonesia's national poverty line is extremely conservative, and the poverty estimates are very sensitive to where the line is drawn. The inequality indices are considered less reliable than the poverty figures. The sample sizes in the smaller provinces are such that the regional poverty figures are at best approximate. Other social indicators, especially quality-based statistics (e.g., educational standards), need to be interpreted with caution. It is of course true that some of the wealthy and well-connected grew very rich (obscenely so in the case of the Soeharto family) over this period. But it is important not to lose sight of the big picture. There is certainly no evidence of growing and widespread inequality or immiserization in the period leading up to the crisis. Life was almost certainly improving for the vast majority of Indonesian citizens.

Secondly, economic growth appeared to be robust. Indonesian economic development was no "myth" in the Krugman (1994) sense of growth being driven almost entirely by factor augmentation rather than total factor productivity (TFP).[4] Among the various TFP estimates, Singapore, not Indonesia, was most commonly singled out as the prime example of "perspiration-led" growth in East Asia. Various estimates placed Indonesia in the mid-range of TFP growth since the 1960s (Chen 1997). Detailed research focused on the country's industrial sector confirmed these results. Moreover, in examining the trends over time, TFP growth appeared to be rising, with slower growth during the oil-financed import substitution era of the 1970s giving way to higher increases in the period of deregulation in the 1980s. Aswicahyono (1998), for example, concluded that non-oil manufacturing TFP grew by 1.1% per annum 1976–80, but 5.5% and 6.0% during 1984–88 and 1989–93 respectively. Timmer (1999) also concluded that TFP grew strongly post-1985, throughout the latter period at more than double that of 1975–85, with especially high growth in the early deregulation years 1986–90.

Thirdly, there was growing political turbulence and uncertainty over this period, but until the middle of 1997 there was no discernible impact on the economy or on any major financial indicators. The years 1996–97 were arguably the most unstable politically since 1967 (Forrester and May 1998). In 1996, the mildly oppositionist Indonesian Democratic Party (PDI) was the subject of ruthless and violent manipulation to ensure that its leader was to the liking of Soeharto. Younger and more radical opponents of the regime were given long gaol sentences. In late 1996 and early 1997 a series of nasty incidents with unpleasant ethnic overtones occurred in several mid-sized Javanese cities. The unrest escalated in the first half of 1997 in West Kalimantan, with extremely violent ethnic conflicts between the indigenous Dayak people and immigrant Madurese (and which occurred again on an even more gruesome scale in March 1999). In May 1997 the election campaign and voting for the Parliament took place, also against a backdrop of unprecedented violence. Then, by the middle of the year, the region's worst ever forest fires occurred, owing to a combination of in-discriminate forest clearing, an unusually long dry season, and lax regulatory supervision. The haze engulfed much of Sumatra and Kalimantan, and also seriously disrupted parts of Malaysia and Singapore.

Nevertheless, these political events had no discernible impact on the economy through to mid-1997. Capital inflows remained buoyant. The stock market was rising. The rupiah continued to bump against the lower limit of the intervention band, and on each occasion the latter was widened the currency quickly appreciated to the new, lower limit. Despite the simmering discontent, the widespread disgust at the business antics of the Soeharto children, and frustration that the much vaunted *keterbukaan* (political openness) of the early 1990s had not materialized, the political protests seemed to abate following the general elections. By July, Soeharto again appeared to be in supreme control.

Finally, almost all available economic and financial indicators looked either buoyant or reasonably comfortable pre-crisis. This is the subject of detailed analysis in Chapter V. To briefly foreshadow our main arguments:

(a) Macroeconomic policy

- Fiscal policy, conventionally defined, was conservative; the budget was broadly in balance, as it had been for some 30 years.
- Inflation was (just) single-digit.

(b) Current account and debt

- The current account deficit appeared manageable, and as a percentage of GDP was less than half that of Thailand in the immediate pre-crisis period
- The external debt to GDP ratio, while quite high, was gradually declining and was appreciably lower than during the difficult adjustment period of the mid 1980s.

(c) Business/efficiency indicators

- Investment and savings were buoyant.
- Indonesia's ICOR was broadly stable in the 1990s and did not register the sharp increase in some of the other crisis economies. (For example, it almost doubled in Thailand and Korea in the course of the decade — see World Bank 1998*b*.)
- Unlike Thailand, in late 1996 and the first half of 1997 there was no evident loss of investor enthusiasm for the rupiah or the stock market.
- Indicators of corporate health appeared broadly satisfactory.
- The construction industry and the urban real estate markets were growing vigorously, but there was no evidence of a major asset price "bubble".
- All major financial ratings exercises for Indonesia continued to be positive, and generally improving. International comparisons (such as the *World Competitiveness Report*) ranked Indonesia rather low compared to the OECD economies, but among emerging markets it assumed an intermediate position, and one which was improving substantially over time. International development agencies as always emphasized the need for further reforms, but their public and semi-official statements gave little hint of an impending crisis.

- There was no generalized wage explosion; real wages in most sectors were rising gradually. Although sharper increases were evident in some high-level international-quality services, the numbers employed were small in aggregate.

(d) Microeconomic/financial reform
- International trade and investment barriers were steadily declining, although the forward momentum had declined since the late 1980s, and several egregious exceptions were much commented upon.
- The process of financial deepening appeared to be progressing steadily, as new financial instruments were introduced; similarly Bank Indonesia's capacity for prudential regulation seemed to be improving.

(e) Balance of payments
- Also unlike Thailand, exchange rate policy was gradually being relaxed, as Bank Indonesia widened its intervention band; there did not appear to be any serious exchange rate misalignment.
- International reserves, both in absolute terms and in months of merchandise imports, were comfortable and rising.
- Export growth showed considerable year-to-year fluctuation in the 1990s, but there was no sudden drop in 1995 and 1996 (World Bank 1998b, p. 20ff).
- Among major East Asian economies, Indonesia was the least exposed to the electronics sector, which appeared to be a significant factor in much of this regional export slowdown. (In its merchandise trade Indonesia was, however, the most exposed to Japan.)

We will return in detail to all these indicators shortly, and show that the problems arose in part because of inadequate information on key indicators and because most observers were not looking at all the relevant variables. But for the present purposes, the main point to emphasize again is the absence of any sense of impending crisis — economic, financial, social, or political — right through to July 1997, followed by a crisis much more severe than that of its neighbours. This is surely one of the key features of the Indonesian experience, and it distinguishes it from all recent crises in East Asia, Latin America, Eastern Europe and Africa. It renders the events of 1997–99 all the more complex and in need of detailed examination.

III

THE COURSE OF THE CRISIS

This chapter examines the course of events from the middle of
1997 to early 1999. By way of backdrop, Figure 1 provides a
summary of the flow of events, Table 1 lists notable economic
and political occurrences over this period, and Figure 2 shows
trends in exchange rates which, in an era of floating regimes,
have proven to be a highly sensitive financial and political
barometer. At the risk of over-simplification, and recognizing

TABLE 1
Chronology of Major Events, July 1997–May 1999

1997	
2/7	Baht floated
21/7	Beginnings … rupiah falls 7%
14/8	Rupiah floated
1/9	First government package announced
16/9	Deferral of major government projects announced
8/10	Government seeks IMF assistance
28/10	"Black Tuesday" on stock market
31/10	Agreement with IMF signed; $38b stand-by facility
1/11	16 banks liquidated
3/11	Detailed reform package announced
17/11	By now clear that Korea is also in serious trouble
4-6/12	Serious Soeharto health rumours; reports that more bank closures imminent

11

TABLE 1 — *continued*

1998

Jan:	Several conflicting estimates of short-term external debt announced; ratings agencies continue to downgrade Indonesia
6/1	Unrealistic budget introduced (assumptions included Rp 4,000, 4% growth, 9% inflation)
8/1	*Washington Post* reports IMF unhappy with reform progress
9/1	Clinton, Hashimoto, etc. call Soeharto
10/1	Rupiah breaks "psychological" 10,000 threshold
13/1	Collapse of Hong Kong's Peregrine, linked to Soeharto's daughter, Tutut
15/1	Second IMF agreement signed; more detailed reform package announced
20/1	Soeharto announces intention to stand for president; Habibie firms as VP favourite
22/1	Rupiah reaches 17,000 to the US dollar; steps to rehabilitate banks announced; creation of IBRA; debt pause requested
23/1	Revised budget announced (Rp 5,000, 0% growth, 20% inflation)
16/2	Government floats intention to establish CBS; BI Governor "dismissed with honour"
5/3	Rift with IMF deepens as deferral of 2nd $3b tranche announced; Rp falls sharply
10/3	MPR elects Soeharto and Habibie as President and Vice President
14/3	Controversial new cabinet announced
20/3	Government announces then quickly withdraws 5% forex tax; CBS proposal officially shelved
30/3	Continuing food protests in several regions
4/4	7 banks closed; 7 more under surveillance
10/4	Third IMF agreement signed
14/4	Minister Bob Hasan: 'this is the Republic of Indonesia, not the IMF Republic'
22/4	IMF disbursements resume

May:	Mounting campus and public protest; 4–5 — cuts to fuel subsidies trigger protests; 12/5 — Trisakti University killings; 14/5 — chaos in Jakarta, 1,000 people killed; exodus of expatriate & ethnic Chinese communities; rupiah falls to below 12,000; students occupy Parliament; 21/5 Soeharto resigns, Habibie installed as third President of Indonesia; new cabinet installed; new IMF talks; 28/5 first major bank (BCA) under IBRA
4/6	Framework established for resolution of private foreign debt
17/6	Rupiah falls to 16,500 amid rising regional uncertainty
25/6	New accord signed with IMF
2/7	INDRA established to tackle private debt
29/7	Fourth IMF agreement signed
30/7	CGI donor consortium provides substantial support
21/8	IBRA takes over several major banks; new bankruptcy law introduced
1/9	Malaysia imposes capital controls and fixes exchange rate; 2/9 Deputy Prime Minister Anwar Ibrahim dismissed
24/9	Paris club debt rescheduling
mid/10	Rupiah strengthens to 6,950 on basis of regional currency shifts and good domestic news; now apparent that threat of hyper-inflation receded
11–13/11	Special MPR session meets; rising political protests culminate in serious violence, renewed looting, and more than 14 deaths.
22/11	Soeharto passes over control of 7 Foundations valued at $530 million; serious violence in Jakarta
30/11	Serious religious/ethnic disturbances in Kupang

1999

5/1	Plausible 1999/2000 budget released; projects 0 growth, 17% inflation, Rp7,500 to the US$.
19/1	Serious week-long ethnic disturbances begin in Ambon; by early March nearly 200 people died
20/1	Rupiah comes under renewed pressure, slips below 9,000
27/2	Government misses bank recap target date; finally announced 13/3

TABLE 1 — *continued*

15/3	Renewal of serious ethnic disturbances in West Kalimantan; more than 200 people killed
22/4	First major bank purchase agreement (Standard Chartered buying 20% of Bank Bali)
23/4	Parliament passes bill increasing local revenue shares in resource-rich provinces
3/5	Release of good economic news: positive growth in Q1 1999 (1.34%); 2nd month of slight deflation

differences among countries, it is possible to identify eight principal sub-phases in the evolution of the crisis.

(i) January–July 1997, beginnings — concern in Thailand

In discussing the course of the crisis, it is useful to distinguish between triggers and fundamental causes. In East Asia the trigger was clearly Thailand, as will be discussed in more detail below. Initially, Indonesia appeared much more robust. "Why Indonesia is not Thailand" (in the words of Tubagus 1997) was a widely held view in mid-1997, and one to which this author was attracted. Around August–September 1997, Indonesia looked better because:

- its authoritarian political system looked better able than Thailand's shaky coalition politics to deliver a clear response to the crisis;
- Bank Indonesia had not squandered its international reserves trying to fight the foreign exchange market;
- its exchange rate regime had not been so rigid;
- it had invited the IMF in advance for "consultation";
- its geo-strategic significance is such that no major country could afford not to participate in a rescue package (in the way that the United States had not signed up to the first Thai package).

(ii) August–October 1997, a wake-up call for the region

The Indonesian government initially seemed to be moving promptly and decisively over most of this period, and at least through until the first half of October 1997 there was still no real indication of what was in store. The rupiah came under sustained selling pressure about three weeks after the baht was floated. The government moved quite quickly, floating the rupiah in mid-August, and introducing minor reform packages in September. It invited the IMF in for "consultation", and by the end of October it had signed on to a package. If anything then the mood was one of cautious optimism. According to one popular school of thought then (to which, again, the author subscribed), the region had been delivered a wake-up call by financial markets, which might — in a relatively painless fashion — curb very high current account deficits, induce governments to clean up the financial sectors, and reign in the proliferating, mostly dubious and off-budget, 'mega-projects'. Moreover, the exchange rate depreciations were delivering greatly increased international competitiveness, which would shift resources back into traded goods activities and accelerate recovery. The concern then, if anything, was that enhanced East Asian competitiveness might quickly trigger a protectionist US response and increased trans-Pacific trade tensions.

(iii) November 1997–January 1998, serious problems evident, Indonesia parts company

November–December: But just as the crisis was not accurately foreseen, so too did this early assessment prove to be excessively sanguine. One might date the really serious beginnings of the crisis — that is, when it was apparent that we had more than a passing "blip" on our hands — from November and December. Over this period, Indonesia's economic and political situation deteriorated sharply. The bank closures of 1 November 1997 triggered widespread uncertainty; backtracking on key reforms to preserve the Soeharto family interests was evident; Korea also joined the casualty list in November; and Soeharto was very ill for a week in early December (at one stage rumours of his death

FIGURE 1
The Crisis in Summary

(1.1) Beginnings

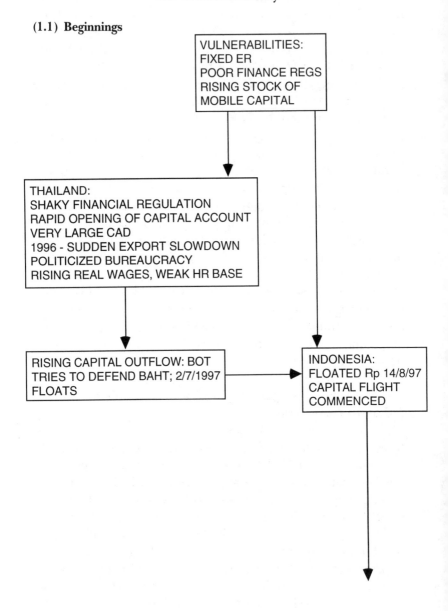

Fig. 1 (*Contd.*)
(1.2) Indonesia in Deep Crisis

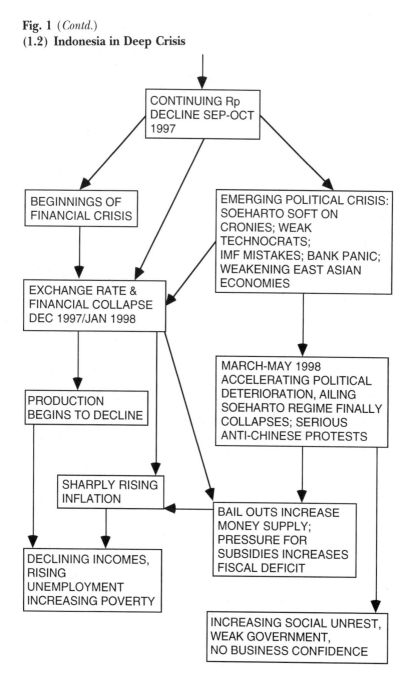

FIGURE 2
Exchange Rate Movements in Southeast Asia, 1997–99
(Local currency/dollar rates, 2 July 1997=100)

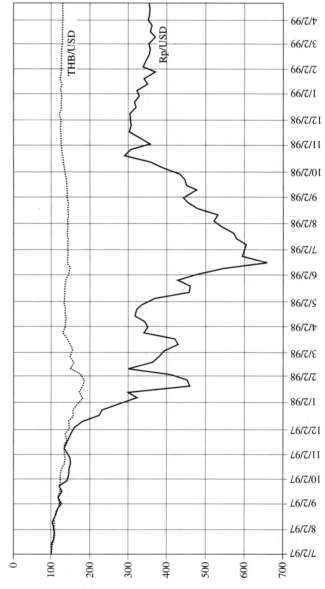

began to circulate). Indonesia then began to part company with the other East Asian crisis economies, as its currency and stock market plummeted to new lows and its financial system virtually ceased to function. The government also began to lose control of the money supply, and hence inflationary pressures quickly surfaced.

January 1998 was a dreadful month, with another round of seriously adverse events (see Table 1): an implausible budget, widening rifts with the IMF (in spite of a high-profile signing ceremony in the middle of the month), and a clear indication that Habibie was set to be elevated to the vice presidency. At one point the rupiah was pushed to as low as 17,000, that is, one-seventh of its pre-crisis level. Even the launching of an "I love the rupiah" movement could not halt the downward spiral!

By then, too, economic activity in Malaysia and the Philippines was slowing down, and even the seemingly impregnable Singaporean economy was coming under pressure. The repercussions for the first time were also becaming global, as financial institutions in Japan, North America and Europe with a significant East Asian exposure came under pressure. One highly publicized casualty was the Hong Kong based Peregrine Securities, which had invested heavily in a Soeharto family enterprise, the Jakarta taxi company Steady Safe.[5]

(iv) February–April 1998, mixed trends

In the next three months of 1998 there were mixed trends. The policy and political uncertainty continued in Indonesia throughout February, as President Soeharto toyed with the highly controversial currency board system (CBS), and then dismissed his respected central bank governor. By now, four critical months had been lost, and there was still no sense of a coherent response to the crisis.

In March and April, a modicum of optimism returned to the region. Exchange rates and stock markets began to pick up a little, especially in Thailand and Malaysia, and even a little in Indonesia. Several factors contributed to this limited improvement. First, in financial markets, an awareness that there had been 'overshooting' triggered some return capital flows in search of assets which, in foreign currency terms, were now extraordinarily cheap. Second, there was a perception that governments were slowly beginning to deal with the policy challenges — there were newly elected governments in Korea and Thailand. The Malaysian administration, and especially its Finance Minister, seemed prepared to enact major reforms. Indonesia's new Cabinet was seriously flawed, with the inclusion of Soeharto's eldest daughter, Tutut, and one of his principal cronies, Bob Hasan (ironically, the first ethnic Chinese in a Soeharto cabinet). But the new economic policy team offered at least a glimmer of hope. Finally, international institutions appeared to be slowly coming to grips with the enormity of the East Asian challenge, and seemed willing to offer assistance in a more flexible and effective manner than was initially the case.

(v) May 1998, The end of the "New Order" — Soeharto toppled

May 1998 will be recorded as a watershed in Indonesian history — the demise of the once seemingly impregnable Soeharto regime. Fuel price increases in early May resulted in a wave of protests. Amid the mounting demonstrations, some students at Jakarta's Trisakti University were shot. This in turn led to a student occupation of the Parliament, a general breakdown in civil order, an exodus of many expatriates and ethnic Chinese, and diminished support for Soeharto among the armed forces and the cabinet. On May 21 these events culminated surprisingly swiftly in the end of the 32-year Soeharto era and the installation of Vice President B.J. Habibie as the Republic's third president.

(vi) June–August 1998, Habibie's shaky beginnings, deepening pessimism

The Habibie administration got off to a shaky start. In the wake of the traumatic events of May, the government was in some respects immobilized and all significant business decisions were put on hold. The Sino-Indonesian community was especially apprehensive following the outbreaks of violence specifically targeting its members. Capital flight continued, and the foreign exchange and stock markets were in the doldrums.

The regional environment was also deteriorating. Japan's economic situation became more precarious. It was apparent that not only was this country incapable of playing a role as the region's economic locomotive, but that it too might be about to join the casualty list. Other problems in the region compounded this sense of crisis: debt work-outs with creditors were (not surprisingly) proving to be extremely complex, there were renewed concerns about policy drift in Thailand, and markets were unsure how the newly installed Estrada administration would perform. During this period it also became apparent that, as a precursor to the introduction of capital controls, Malaysia was moving away from its de facto "IMF-like" policy approach.

(vii) September–December 1998, renewed, cautious optimism

By late September, a modicum of optimism was again returning to the region, based principally on a perception that the worst may have passed. In Indonesia, the Habibie Administration survived its first 100 days, and most of the new political actors were displaying a sense of pragmatism on economic policy issues. The rupiah strengthened to below 7,500 for the first time in more than six months, and thus appeared to be entering a range broadly considered to be "manageable". The international donor pledges in late July were deemed to have given the country's fiscal position much-needed credibility. Inflation in September fell to 3.75%, which was well down on the previous four months. A good crop was bringing rice prices down. Non-oil exports were holding up reasonably well. Elsewhere in the region, the beneficial effects of Japanese restructuring and reflation appeared (weakly) evident. Capital was beginning to return to most of the crisis economies.

(viii) January–April 1999, mixed trends again

The hopeful signs emerging in late 1998 continued into 1999. The 1999 worst-case projections for any major economy in East

Asia were now a contraction for Indonesia in the range 2–5%. Korea's prospects looked encouraging, Thailand was slowly resolving its financial restructuring and legal bottlenecks, and Malaysia's experiment with capital controls was not proving as disastrous as had been feared initially. In the first quarter of 1999, Indonesia again returned — unexpectedly — to positive economic growth, and inflation was slightly negative in March and April. Nevertheless, the country's immediate prospects were clouded by uncertainty. Export performance continued to be very poor. The commercial climate was dominated by a perception that all major economic policy decisions were on-hold until after the general and presidential elections. Continuing ethnic and religious violence also deterred investors. Moreover, it was not clear that the regional crisis was definitely over. Japan in particular was still poised precariously.

IV

SOCIO-ECONOMIC IMPACTS

Owing to the frustratingly slow release of relevant data, it is still too early to be precise about the social impacts of the crisis. But economic and financial statistics are readily available, and the broad social picture is clear enough. We consider each of these in turn.

Economic Indicators

Indonesia is by far the worst affected Southeast Asian economy. Its economy contracted by 13.6% in 1998, about double that of Malaysia and Thailand (Table 2). It was also the only economy to experience serious inflation in 1998. Its current account adjustment in 1997–98 was very large, equivalent to over 8 percentage points of GDP. However, since it was running a smaller deficit pre-crisis than either Malaysia or Thailand, the magnitude of the adjustment in the latter two countries was actually larger. If one takes 1996 as the last "normal" year for Thailand, its adjustment — 16% of GDP — was exceptionally large. The change in Indonesia's fiscal policy stance was similar to its neighbours. As the country deepest in crisis, it is not surprising that it is running the largest fiscal deficit.

The gravity of Indonesia's situation is appreciated immediately once it is placed in some sort of comparative historical context. In the 30 years from 1967, the country averaged about 6.5% annual growth and, depending on which base one chooses for

23

TABLE 2
Southeast Asian Economic Indicators, 1991–98
(In percentages)

	Ind	Mal	Phil	Sing	Thai	VN
GDP growth:						
1991–5	7.8	8.7	2.2	8.5	8.6	8.2
1996	8.0	8.6	5.5	6.9	5.5	9.4
1997	4.7	8.0	5.1	7.8	–0.4	9.0
1998	–13.6	–6.7	0	1.3	–6.5	5.0
Inflation:						
1991–5	8.9	3.6	10.5	2.6	4.8	23.4
1996	6.5	3.5	8.4	1.4	5.8	4.5
1997	11.6	2.6	5.1	2.0	5.6	4.0
1998	65.0	5.4	9.0	–0.2	8.1	5.0
Current Account/GDP:						
1991–5	–2.4	–7.0	–3.6	12.9	–6.2	–5.5
1996	–3.3	–4.9	–4.5	15.0	–7.9	–16.2
1997	–2.9	–5.2	–5.2	15.4	–2.0	–8.6
1998	5.4	7.5	1.2	17.8	8.1	
Govt Balance/GDP:						
1991–5	–0.2	0.3	–1.6	12.4	2.8	–3.5
1996	1.2	1.1	–0.4	13.9	2.4	–0.4
1997	1.2	5.5	–1.8	6.0	–0.9	
1998	–5.5	–1.0	–3.6	–1.0	–4.5	

Sources: Asia Pacific Economics Group, *Asia Pacific Profiles 1998*
(Canberra, 1998); IMF, *World Economic Outlook*; JP Morgan, "World
Financial Markets", First Quarter 1999; press reports.

the national accounts series, there was either no, or at most one,
year of (slightly) negative growth over this period. Thus, some
two-thirds of the population have no experience of a recession,
let alone the dramatic plunge which has occurred. A decline in
per capita GDP of about 15.5% in the context of a long-term
average annual expansion of 4.5% implies that the 1998 crisis
"cost" Indonesia some 3.5 years of growth, and returned it to

levels prevailing in 1994–95. Assuming also that Indonesia experiences subdued growth for the next few years, the longer term cost of the crisis will of course be a good deal greater, in terms of its departure from the pre-crisis high-growth trajectory. In historical regional context, Indonesia's economic contraction in 1998 was larger than the *combined effect* of the decline which occurred in the Philippines' two worst crisis years 1985 and 1986, surrounding the demise of Ferdinand Marcos. Going back further in history, the fall in GDP in 1998 was larger than that which occurred in any year of the great depression in the United Kingdom, and was equivalent to two-thirds of the *aggregate* decline in the years 1929–32 (Arndt 1944, p. 22). At current exchange rates (which of course give a misleading picture), Indonesia has suddenly gone from being the largest among the five original ASEAN member countries to the smallest.

As would be expected, the sectoral effects of the crisis have been very uneven, and the aggregate figure masks large inter-sectoral differences (see Table 3).[6] In particular, agricultural output has been virtually constant, whereas the decline in the construction and finance sectors has been quite dramatic. A number of factors have contributed to the relatively buoyant situation in agriculture from about the middle of 1998. The breaking of the El Nino-induced drought mid-year produced good dry season food crops; but for the drought, agricultural output would have been more strongly positive. The gradual removal of food subsidies and price controls increased returns to farmers. The export-oriented cash crop sector benefited from the rupiah depreciation, which more than outweighed low international prices.

Other major sectors have fallen between the extremes of agriculture and construction. Manufacturing has contracted at about the economy-wide average, but with major differences between export-oriented and local market activities. The export-oriented mining sector has been affected by low international commodity prices. The decline in the government sector highlights the fact that fiscal policy has been only weakly counter-cyclical.

TABLE 3
GDP Growth by Sector, 1995–98
(In percentages)

	1995	1996	1997	1998
Agriculture	4.2	1.9	0.7	0.2
Mining & Quarrying	6.6	7.1	1.7	–4.2
Manufacturing	6.7	11.0	6.4	–12.9
Utilities	15.5	12.6	12.8	3.7
Construction	12.9	12.4	6.4	–39.7
Trade, hotel, restaurant	7.7	7.6	5.8	–19.0
Transport & communication	9.4	8.6	8.3	–12.8
Finance	13.6	9.9	7.2	–37.6
Accommodation	5.5	6.8	5.0	–20.7
Public administration	1.3	1.3	1.2	–7.0
Other services	9.3	8.8	5.7	–0.9
GDP	8.2	7.8	4.9	–13.7

Note: 1998 data are preliminary.
Source: BPS.

As the world's largest archipelagic state, Indonesia's regional dynamics have altered significantly during the crisis. At the time of writing, no new regional accounts data had been released, but the broad picture is clear enough. This has been a crisis first and foremost of the modern, urban economy of Java. Greater Jakarta (Jabotabek), with its reliance on formal sector manu-facturing, modern services, a large construction industry, and the public sector, is experiencing a painful contraction. By contrast, many of the hitherto poor and neglected provinces east of Bali are doing quite well. The distant province of North Sulawesi, for example, with its strong cash crop sector and good human capital base is said to be one of the few provinces which may have experienced positive growth in 1998. Bali, the fastest growing province during the Soeharto era, has been affected by the downturn in tourism, but it is unlikely to have declined as sharply as Java. Provinces such as these two, with a record of more relaxed social relations, are said to be attracting some of the ethnic Chinese community's financial and human resources.

There have been even more pronounced variations among the major expenditure groups (Table 4). The decline in household consumption was quite modest, for a number of reasons related to various survival strategies. The dramatic wealth losses associated with the demise of the stock market had little impact on personal consumption, presumably because stock holdings are still limited mainly to a small urban elite. By contrast, the crisis hit investment and inventories very hard, and both collapsed. Government consumption declined at about the same rate as the economy as a whole, and underlines again the absence of a fiscal stimulus.[7] Exports rose modestly, while imports contracted, though not as much as might have been expected. Since both are foreign currency denominated, allowance must be made for the large rupiah depreciation in 1998.

These figures provide a number of clues about the welfare effects of the crisis. Agriculture is still by far the largest jobs provider (see Table 8 below), and thus the welfare of this largest single group in the community has not been adversely affected *directly*. "Other services" contains much of the informal sector

TABLE 4
Growth of Expenditure on GDP, 1995–98

	1995	1996	1997	1998
Household consumption	9.7	9.2	6.6	−2.9
Government consumption	1.3	3.8	0.1	−14.4
Gross Fixed capital formation	14.0	12.2	8.6	−40.9
Change in stock	7.3	−9.9	25.8	−137.1
Exports of goods & services	8.5	7.6	7.8	10.6
Imports of goods & services	27.1	6.9	14.7	−5.4

Note: 1998 data are preliminary.
Source: BPS.

activities, and here the decline has been slight. The modest fall in household consumption also suggests that, in aggregate, community living standards fell much less than that implied by the decline in GDP. Export growth rose, to the benefit of those deriving income from this sector. This varied outlook is important in assessing social impacts, an issue we address shortly.

We can trace the monetary impacts of the crisis by observing monthly data on money supply, inflation and interest rates over the period 1996–98. These are shown in Figures 3 and 4. Money supply is represented by base money, while the CPI is used for inflation; both are presented as series with January 1996=100. Interest rates are represented by Bank Indonesia Certificates (SBIs) and 3-month time deposits. The origins of the sudden bout of inflation are clearly evident in the base money series, which suddenly increased sharply (by 36% on a month-on-month

FIGURE 3
Inflation and Money Supply, 1996–98
(Monthly data, Jan 1996=100)

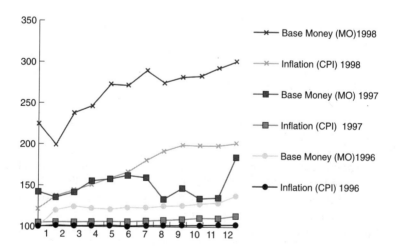

Source: Bank Indonesia.

basis) in December 1997 and January 1998 (22%); in May 1998 it rose a further 11%. All three months coincided with bank bail-outs or runs.[8] From May 1998 onwards, the government regained control of the money supply, and it rose by just 7.5% over the next six months.

Inflation followed these trends very closely, with a lag. The first appreciable increase was December 1997 (3%), jumping quickly to 7% and 13% respectively in January and February 1998. From March to September, inflation was high though around a gradually declining trend. It then flattened out quite suddenly, and in the seven months from October Indonesia was suddenly almost inflation-free, the CPI rising just 5.2%. The prospect of hyper-inflation receded swiftly — monetary orthodoxy works quickly! Interest rates also began to respond promptly, albeit with a lag. SBIs almost trebled January–April 1998, and

FIGURE 4
Interest Rates, 1996–98
(Monthly data, %)

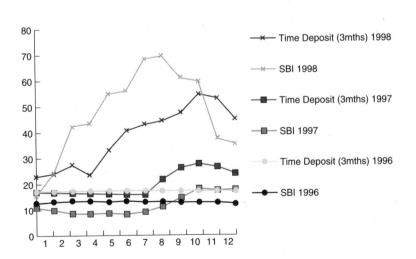

Source: Bank Indonesia.

rose a further 50% to July, before declining quite sharply in November. Time deposits moved in the same direction, but with a further lag. In a period of rapidly fluctuating inflation rates, and great uncertainty, it is not easy to measure real interest rates, since the results will vary considerably depending on the choice of rates, deflators and inflationary expectations. However, it would be difficult to sustain the argument of excessive monetary tightening over this period. By practically any measure, real interest rates were negative throughout 1998. The low inflation appeared to be secure by April 1999, as the proposed fiscal deficit for FY 1999/2000 should be very nearly covered by foreign aid, and the bank recapitalization costs will be kept mainly off-budget (apart from the 'carrying costs' of the special bonds, to be funded partly from the receipts from privatization). Thus, interest rates should continue to fall, if not fully to pre-crisis levels, owing to increased risk premia.

The balance of payments provide an additional dimension to this picture of economic collapse (Table 5). As noted, the current account turned from deficit to surplus quickly, primarily owing to the collapse of imports, which fell by about $15 billion compared to pre-crisis levels. One of the disappointing features of the crisis has been the poor performance of exports, which in dollar terms actually declined in 1998/99. Some 60% of this decline occurred in the oil/gas sector, and was beyond the country's control as it reflected historically low international prices. But non-oil exports also declined (though not, as noted above, in real rupiah terms), and here also Indonesia's record was inferior to that of its neighbours. There was a terms of trade effect at work in both agriculture and manufactures, the latter especially the result of the severe price competition from newly competitive neighbours. This factor, too, was common to the other crisis economies.

Indonesia's especially weak export performance related to a combination of additional factors:

- cancelled orders owing to supply uncertainties;
- the suspension of trade credit associated with the banking

TABLE 5
Indonesia's Balance of Payments, 1995/96–1998/99
(US$ billions)

	1995/6	1996/7	1997/8	1998/9
(1) **Current a/c**	–7.0	–8.1	–1.7	4.5
Exports	47.8	52.0	56.2	50.7
imports	41.5	45.8	42.7	30.9
services (net)	13.2	14.3	15.2	15.3
Non–oil/gas (net)	–0.5	–1.9	7.3	15.5
exports	37.1	39.3	45.9	43.6
imports	37.6	41.1	38.6	28.1
Oil/gas (net)	10.8	8.1	6.2	4.3
exports	14.7	12.8	10.3	7.1
imports	3.9	4.7	4.1	2.8
(2) **Capital a/c**	11.5	12.7	–7.6	4.4
Official capital	–0.2	–0.8	4.2	15.2
inflows	5.7	5.3	8.3	10.6
amortization	–5.9	–6.1	–4.1	–4.0
exceptional funding			3.0	8.6
Private capital	11.7	13.5	–11.8	–10.8
FDI	5.4	6.5	1.8	–0.9
others	6.3	6.9	–13.7	–9.9
Total	4.5	4.6	–9.3	8.9
Errors & Omissions	–1.8	–0.7	–0.7	1.0
Monetary movements	–2.7	–3.9	10.0	–9.9
Official reserves (end period)	16.0	19.9	16.5	26.4

Note: 1998/99 data are preliminary estimates.
Source: Bank Indonesia.

sector collapse, and fears that Bank Indonesia would not be able to honour letters of credit;

- shipping bottlenecks following the sharp fall in imports;
- its greater exposure to the weak Japanese economy;
- supply disruptions owing to localized outbreaks of looting and poor law and order; and
- the reduced presence of (the more export-oriented) MNCs in the country.

With the collapse of investment, and government slow to inject a fiscal stimulus, much hangs on the export response. Unfortunately, these problems, at this critical juncture in history, have slowed the pace of economic recovery.

The capital account mirrors in part these trends in the current account. It turned negative in the first crisis year, 1998–98 because private capital movements changed so dramatically, from a net inflow of $13.5 billion to an outflow of $11.8 billion, and because official inflows obviously could not respond with the same speed. By 1998–99, the capital account is estimated to have turned positive again, thanks to large official flows, grossing $19.2 billion. However, private capital flows continued to be large and negative, even through until the last quarter of calendar year 1998, suggesting that business confidence is still very weak. Even foreign direct investment (FDI) was negative which, as we will show shortly, is another factor setting Indonesia apart from the other crisis economies. The combination of positive current and capital accounts augmented Indonesia's reserves, which had fallen considerably during the worst of the crisis months.

Financial Indicators

Stock markets and exchange rates fell sharply in the crisis economies, and here also Indonesia has fared much worse than its neighbours since mid 1997, and especially since about November of that year. Whereas some of the other countries' currencies began to recover in the first half of 1998 from their initial over-shooting, Indonesia's market continued to be very low until the last quarter of 1998 (Figure 2). As Table 6 documents, from 1 July 1997 to the beginning of 1998 and to the first quarter of 1999 the rupiah fell much further against the US dollar than any other internationally traded East Asian currency. By 31 March 1999, its nominal value was just 28% of that in mid-1997, less than half that of the region-wide average and any other crisis economy. The data also illustrate that Indonesia's currency has been much slower to rebound from the lows of early 1998 than its neighbours. These exchange rate movements initially translated into a much sharper real depreciation than in the other crisis economies, and for 1998 as a whole. But by the end of the year, the nominal appreciation in the last quarter, combined with the country's much higher inflation, had eroded a good deal of these gains in competitiveness. Indonesia's real depreciation from 1990 to the end of 1998, for example, was about the same as Korea's, although the fall in Indonesia 1996–98 was sharper.

The decline in Indonesia's stock market in local currency terms was initially broadly similar to the crisis economies, but it displayed very little recovery through to early 1999, a feature it shared (for different reasons) with both Malaysia and Thailand. Owing principally to currency movements, Indonesia's stock market decline in US dollar terms has been by far the greatest over this period. By March 31 1999 its stock market index was still just 15% of that in mid-1997. The next two worst performers, Malaysia and Thailand were still about double and triple Indonesia in this respect. The market capitalization of the Jakarta Stock Exchange declined from about $100 billion pre-crisis to some $11 billion by end-September 1998. Some of the stock market declines have been truly spectacular, with a few companies' market capitalization having been effectively wiped out.[9]

The large flight of mobile capital from Indonesia is not surprising given the panic of 1997 and the political turbulence and social tension of 1998. However, what is in some respects more worrying still is the trend in FDI, which responds to longer-term and more sober assessments of an economy's prospects

TABLE 6
Comparative Financial Data, 1997–99

(a) Exchange rate (/$) (indexed at 30/6/97=100)	1/1/97	30/6/97	1/1/98	31/3/99
China	100	100	100	100
India	100	100	90	84
Indonesia	103	100	30	28
Korea	105	100	51	73
Malaysia	100	100	56	66
Philippines	100	100	58	68
Singapore	102	100	82	83
Taiwan	101	100	81	84
Thailand	102	100	48	67

(b) REERs (1990 =100, period averages)	1996	1997	1998	12/1998
India	75	82	80	77
Indonesia	104	95	46	71
Korea	89	83	66	71
Malaysia	111	108	83	82
Philippines	115	109	91	96
Singapore	115	117	113	109
Taiwan	89	90	87	92
Thailand	106	97	88	99

(c) Stock market index (in local currency; indexed at 30/6/97=100)	1/1/97	30/6/97	1/1/98	31/3/99
China	70	100	97	91
India	80	100	90	90
Indonesia	89	100	55	55
Korea	92	100	58	88
Malaysia	116	100	49	47
Philippines	112	100	62	71
Singapore	110	100	68	75
Taiwan	77	100	87	77
Thailand	168	100	75	73

Table 6 — *continued*

(d) Stock market index (in $; indexed at 30/6/97=100)	1/1/97	30/6/97	1/1/98	31/3/99
China	70	100	97	91
India	80	100	81	76
Indonesia	92	100	17	15
Korea	97	100	29	64
Malaysia	115	100	27	31
Philippines	113	100	36	49
Singapore	112	100	56	62
Taiwan	79	100	71	65
Thailand	165	100	36	49

Notes: Stock market and nominal exchange rate data refer to the nearest weekly closing figures for the date indicated. Upward movements in exchange rate series refer to appreciation.
Sources: Economist, various issues, for stock market and nominal exchange rate data; JP Morgan for real effective exchange rates.

(Table 7). Here Indonesia is a complete outlier among the five East Asian crisis economies. From being the largest recipient of FDI in 1996, and nearly so in 1997, it is estimated to have been the only one to experience a net outflow in 1998. The contrast with the two other economies under an IMF crisis programme is particularly noticeable, since FDI inflows to both almost doubled. They underline again that Indonesia's situation is much more precarious, that East Asia's large cash-rich 'Chinese' investors (i.e., Hong Kong, Singapore, and Taiwan) are shunning Indonesia, and that its recovery will be much slower.

Social Indicators

Assessments of the social impact of the crisis vary wildly. At one extreme is an alarmist estimate by a major international agency that about one-half of the population is now in poverty (ILO 1998), to upbeat assessments suggesting the "rebirth" of a newly invigourated people's economy. Jellinek and Rustanto (1999 pp. 1–2) provide an example of the latter:

TABLE 7
FDI Flows to the Asian Crisis Economies, 1991–98
(US$ billions)

	1991–5 (ave)	1996	1997	1998
Indonesia	2.3	6.2	4.7	−1.3
Korea	1.0	2.3	2.8	5.1
Malaysia	4.5	5.1	5.1	3.6
Philippines	1.0	1.5	1.1	1.0
Thailand	1.9	2.3	3.7	7.0

Note: 1998 data are estimates.
Source: UNCTAD, FDI/TNC database, Geneva.

Indonesia's informal sector has picked up the slack and seems to be experiencing an economic boom. ... Small enterprises, killed off during 20 years of economic boom of the New Order, are being revived. Old traditions of artisanship and trade are being rediscovered. Rich and middle class consumers who formerly bought from the formal sector are now buying from traditional markets. ...
In contrast to the economic crash depicted in the official, national and international media, we are witnessing an unprecedented economic boom in the small-scale sector.

Both these conclusions are misleading in important respects, the former because the estimation procedures were flawed, the latter because a return to activities characterized by low productivity and incomes hardly constitutes good news. In fact, all available evidence suggests that social outcomes have been between these two extremes. Many people have obviously been hurt by the crisis, but the severity of the social impacts has been overstated.

These disagreements have arisen in part because, in contrast to the economic-financial data, which provide a reasonably accurate picture of the crisis, social trends are much more difficult to estimate with any precision. Quick-release, comprehensive data on poverty, unemployment, education, health and nutrition are rarely available at the best of times. During a period of crisis, social dislocation and inflation they are all the more problematic. One wants to know not only the aggregate trends, but also the position of vulnerable groups (e.g., the low-skilled, the urban unemployed, children, women, those in traditionally very poor regions). And, as important as the overall figures, there needs to be an analytical understanding of the adaptive and survival strategies of the poor and 'near-poor'. This includes their capacity to adjust consumption patterns (e.g., deferring the purchase of consumer durable goods, switching to nutritionally more cost-effective food sources); to draw on savings, remittances, and extended family networks; and also their ability to shift to new employment opportunities either sectorally or spatially.

In addition, many middle class households have had some dollar-denominated assets. For example, dollar bank accounts pre-crisis were quite common in Indonesia; subsequently of course they have proliferated. Moreover, compositional changes are also important. Beneath the aggregate poverty figures, there is known to be considerable "turnover" in poverty incidence, as people move in and out of poverty. This is especially so during the current crisis, with its highly uneven sectoral and spatial impacts. Finally, in a new, highly politicized environment, one does not have to be excessively cynical to observe that powerful vested interests exist with a stake in either overstating or understating the seriousness of the situation.

An assessment of social trends is also sensitive to selection of time periods and to the impact of unrelated, non-crisis phenomena. Through until early 1998, the rural poor were affected much more by the drought, which resulted in below-average agricultural growth in 1997 (Table 3). The government maintained food subsidies, partly through rice imports at a special exchange rate of Rp 5,000, for several months into 1998. In addition there were subsidies for fuel, electricity and some other "essentials". Moreover, many firms made an effort to maintain their workforce during the first 6–9 months of the crisis, at least until the end of fasting month in late January 1998.

It is perhaps not surprising, therefore, that the estimates of poverty incidence vary so widely, and why general social assessments range from the alarmist to the cautiously optimistic. One's approach depends not only upon the general view of "development", and how it should be measured, but also upon which particular socio-economic "snippets" are being more intensively observed. The export-oriented cash crop farmer in Sulawesi and the displaced Jakarta construction worker will present a very different picture! Indeed, some writers view the developments of 1997–99 very positively, as the birth of a new development era, as the quote above from Jellinek and Rustanto (1999) illustrates: the poor are not suffering greatly, it is alleged, owing to the resilience of the agricultural and informal sectors; while the crisis presents Indonesia with a historic opportunity to rid itself of crony-dominated, corrupt, capitalist-style development.

The labour force data provide one reasonably clear indication of social impacts, although one must be cautious in drawing strong inferences from just two, point-to-point observations. Early reports suggested that the unemployment rate was rising sharply, from less than 5% to over 20%, with underemployment rising equally rapidly. However, in an economy like Indonesia, labour market adjustments invariably take the form of transfers to informal sector activities and reduced earnings, rather than open unemployment (Manning 1999). The Sakernas labour force survey data conducted in August 1997 (essentially pre-crisis) and 1998 (well into the crisis) reported very little change in either open unemployment or underemployment (Table 8). These figures appear implausibly low, especially the suggested *decline* in underemployment, but they do at least correct the earlier, more sensational conjectures.

The employment data also suggest substantial sectoral mobility one year into the crisis (Table 8). Agriculture's share is reported to have risen 10% (or more than four percentage points), and it accommodated more than double the increment to the workforce over these 12 months.[10] Every other sector shed labour, with the biggest decline occurring in manufacturing. The

TABLE 8
Labour Market Adjustment, 1997–98

	1997	*1998*
% unemployed	4.7	5.5
% underemployed	12.0	9.3
Work-force by sector (% of total):		
agriculture	40.7	45.0
mining	1.0	0.8
manufacturing	12.9	11.3
construction	4.9	4.0
trade & tourism	19.9	19.2
transport & communication	4.8	4.7
finance & accommodation	0.8	0.7
govt & private services	14.7	14.1
Labour productivity (major sectors, Rp '000, 1993 prices):		
all sectors	5,083	3,966
agriculture	1,848	1,635
manufacturing	9,885	9,544
construction	8,373	5,996
trade & tourism	4,336	3,543
transport & communication	7,798	6,753
finance & accommodation	58,977	45,924
govt & private services	2,994	2,894
Contribution to employment expansion, 1997–98 (% of total):		
agriculture	204	
mining	–8.9	
manufacturing	–47.4	
utilities	–3.8	
construction	–29.3	
trade & tourism	–6.1	
transport & communications	1.2	
finance & accommodation	–1.7	
govt & private services	–8.0	
(absolute expansion = 2,266.9 thousand)		

Note: Underemployment is defined as those in the work-force, working less than 35 hours per week, and seeking additional employment.
Source: Badan Pusat Statistik, *Sakernas*, August 1997 & 1998.

comparative labour productivity estimates presented in the table also give some crude indication of the flexibility of these sectors' factor proportions (and hence their labour-absorptive capacity) during the crisis. Manufacturing and other services (the latter dominated by public sector employment) emerge as the least flexible sectors, and construction the most. Productivity in agriculture fell but, contrary to expectations, not by as much as that in most service sectors.

Various estimates of real wages suggest a significant decline, but one which varies according to region and sector, and is sensitive to the choice of deflator (Manning 1999). Those in rice agriculture on Java fell by about 30–50% during 1998. Non-agricultural activities were generally worse affected, particularly sectors such as construction and import-substituting manufacturing. By contrast, the decline in agriculture off-Java was probably less, and in some buoyant sectors (e.g., cash-crop agriculture) it is possible that they were roughly constant. In the case of the latter, the benefits of increased international competitiveness accrued directly to plantation owners and small-holders, and so will not necessarily be reflected in the wage data.[11]

As noted, the poverty estimates are the most controversial, but the most plausible set of estimates suggest a modest increase. Immediately before the crisis, about 11% of the population was estimated to be below the official poverty line. A priori, if per capita incomes have fallen back to about 1994 levels, the starting point in the analysis would be to assume that poverty incidence would resemble the figure of that year, or some 13% of the population. In fact, it might even be expected to be slightly lower than this. Poverty estimates are generally expenditure-based, and the decline in real per capita household consumption in 1998 was very similar to the increase in the previous year, suggesting that perhaps 1996 might be the relevant benchmark guesstimate.

These are averages for the whole country. One might also hypothesize that income and expenditure inequality fell somewhat during the crisis, since the better off are more likely to derive their income from the modern urban economy, which has registered the sharpest decline (not to mention the collapse on the stock market and in "top-end" real estate), whereas the poor are more likely to work in the relatively resilient agricultural and informal sectors. Thus, it is even conceivable that the increase in poverty could be less still. All this is very approximate, of course and, pending the arrival of better data, must remain speculative. But, as with unemployment, if nothing else this back-of-the-envelope reasoning demonstrates that some of the early alarmist estimates are quite unreliable.

Three major sets of poverty estimates for 1998 and 1999 had been prepared by early 1999, and their results vary wildly (Table 9). The most reliable and rigorous are those prepared by Poppele, Sumarto and Pritchett (1999). They base their findings on three data sources, covering the months August–September 1997 and 1998: the ongoing Indonesian Family Life Survey (IFLS) collected by Rand and the University of Indonesia's Demographic Institute; a "100-village survey" undertaken by BPS and UNICEF; and a qualitative Kecamatan Crisis Impact Survey, also conducted by BPS. A resample of the first data base, involving almost 2,000 households in seven provinces, constitutes their main source of information.

TABLE 9
Estimates of Poverty Incidence
(% of population)

		Urban	Rural	Total
BPS	1993	13.4	13.8	13.7
	1996	9.7	12.3	11.3
	1998 (June)	28.8	45.6	39.1
ILO	1998 (Dec.)	39.1	53.2	48.2
	1999 (Dec.)	56.6	71.7	66.3
Poppele et al.	1998 (A)	12.0	15.2	13.8
	1998 (B)	15.8	23.0	19.9

Sources: ILO (1998), Poppele et al. (1999), and unpublished data from BPS.

The authors' findings of a small rise in poverty incidence are generally consistent with the expectations adumbrated above. The study also concluded that between 1997 and 1998 there was a strong inverse correlation between education levels and the rise in poverty. That is, those with little or no formal education, although registering the highest poverty incidence, experienced very little increase in poverty. The percentage increase in poverty then rises for each completed education level (primary, secondary, tertiary). Such a finding lends additional support to the prima facie hypothesis that inter-personal inequality has declined during the crisis.

All three sources are at best approximate, but the earlier estimates prepared by the ILO and BPS greatly overstate the incidence of poverty.[12] The ILO figures are the most flawed methodologically, since they were based on an inflation rate of 80% (fairly close to the mark) but allowed for no rise in nominal incomes. In fact, nominal wages rose appreciably in all sectors although, depending on which deflator is chosen, real wages may have fallen by as much as 40% (Manning 1999; Cameron 1999; pp. 16–17). Real agricultural earnings may have actually increased through the year: in the case of food crops when the drought broke and rice prices were lifted to international levels, and in the case of export-oriented cash crops as the exchange rate depreciation began to feed through to producers. BPS estimates apparently allowed for some increase in nominal wages, but assumed incorrectly that poorer groups would be most affected by the crisis.[13]

These results are also highly sensitive to the choice of deflator, as the estimates of Poppele et al. (1999) demonstrate. Their estimate (A) employs BPS province-specific deflators, which are presumably the most reliable. An alternative series (B) is based on an IFLS estimate of the price movements for 38 consumption items. This produces a higher inflation rate and therefore, given the same increase in nominal expenditures, a larger increase in poverty. However, it is still well below the ILO and BPS figures, and as the authors argue there is no compelling reason for preferring the IFLS deflator to those prepared by BPS.

Education indicators present a mixed picture. Enrolment ratios fell slightly in 1998, by about 1.6% in both primary and junior secondary schools (MOEC/World Bank 1999). In the case of the latter, urban enrolments fell more sharply, confirming the impression that the urban economy has been hardest hit. Private school figures appear to be worse affected than government schools, reflecting the relative costs of the two systems, and also the partial success of the government's campaign to abolish entry fees (but not the many other informal levies) at these two levies. Thus the data suggest that the educational impacts of the crisis have been largely contained, but more comprehensive data are obviously required to confirm such a conclusion.[14]

There are as yet no comprehensive data on other social indicators, which are in any case even more difficult to monitor. Nation-wide, quick-release health data are not available. Unpublished UNICEF data, based on hospital surveys, suggest some increase in infant and maternal mortality, and in the incidence of diarrhoeal diseases. It is reasonable to surmise that rising costs in the modern health sector have put these services beyond the reach of many. But this sector catered mainly to the urban middle class anyway, and so the effects are probably limited. Modern pharmaceuticals have risen in price, since their manufacture is highly import-intensive, but the increases have been cushioned owing to subsidies and a switch to generic products. Similarly, the reported incidence of malnutrition has been rising, but by how much is not yet clear. It is arguably the case that the drought had a more serious impact on food availability than the financial crisis, certainly in rural areas, and that the good rains since mid-1998 have alleviated these pressures. The principal challenge here too relates to those in the urban economy who have experienced a sharp fall in real incomes, and who have only limited access to traditional support mechanisms in rural areas.

There are no reliable data on the impact of the crisis among the various size groups of enterprises At the behest of the Minister for Co-operatives and Small Enterprise, Adi Sasono, the government has introduced a range of subsidized credit programs for this group, arguing that they are the key to economic recovery, social cohesion and *pribumi* advancement, and therefore warrant support. But anecdotal evidence does suggest that SMEs are weathering the storm somewhat better than many larger firms. This is to be expected: they are generally less exposed to the modern financial sector; they tend to produce "necessities" rather than "luxuries"; and they are generally more nimble and less burdened by expensive overheads. Indeed, as noted, Jellinek and Rustanto (1999) argued that Central Java's informal sector is flourishing during the crisis. Many SMEs are closely linked to the agricultural sector, in processing and distribution activities, and most of these are presumably doing quite well. A case study of SME furniture producers in the town of Jepara (north coast of Central Java) by Sandee and Andadari (1998) concluded that these firms were actually expanding during the crisis. Nevertheless, it may simply be that export orientation is the key to success during the crisis, and that this — more than scale — is the critical variable in the Jepara case study.

In addition to these quantifiable indicators, there are frequent media and anecdotal reports of dislocation, hardship and violence among local communities and families. The state of law and order certainly appears to have deteriorated markedly. Crime is reported to be rising sharply. "Jakarta: City of Fear" was the perhaps overly-dramatic headline of a *Jakarta Post* edition in January 1999. Looting of containers in the ports, factories and shops is souring the commercial environment. Attempts have been made to partially appropriate some private plantations in Sulawesi. There are frequent reports about disputes over land, while government offices at all tiers of the administration have been attacked. The dominant ethnic Chinese business community continues to be a prime target, but it is by no means the only one. No doubt rising poverty and unemployment have been a factor in all this. Political paybacks have been another factor in the equation, as those who felt mistreated by officialdom during the Soeharto era have sought to level the score. In addition, the widely reviled police force (as distinct from the armed forces, which continue to command somewhat more respect) has been unable to preserve local order in a number of locations.

Thus, in sum, piecing together the disparate elements of the social impacts picture is a complex task. The truth is somewhere between the diverging assessments of widespread, deep poverty, and glowing accounts of rural and informal sector growth and prosperity. There has not been the mass poverty which was earlier anticipated, although groups of individuals in particular regions and sectors have experienced great hardship. Conversely, while many in the agricultural and informal sectors have experienced no great hardship, and possibly even an increase in real incomes, it needs to be remembered that these are generally low productivity and income activities, and that the rapid economic growth and structural change of the past three decades had drawn millions of Indonesians into higher-income alternatives.

In effect, a process of "involution" is taking place, which offers some short-term relief during the crisis, but it is certainly not the basis for sustained socio-economic development. The deterioration in living standards is serious but not catastrophic, providing growth is quickly restored. The longer the recession lasts, the more the capital stock built up over the last 30 years of rapid growth will deteriorate. In the process, more people will be pushed below the poverty line, and the various short-term adjustment and "coping" mechanisms will become less effective. The contraction in household expenditure was just one-fifth of that of the overall economy in 1998, but such a "cushioning" is necessarily just a once-off phenomenon.

V

CAUSES OF THE CRISIS ·

We come now to the major puzzle of the episode: why did it happen? This broad question immediately points to a number of specific questions:

- Why was the crisis so severe (and not, for example, a relatively mild correction)?
- Were the crisis economies, Indonesia in particular, 'accidents waiting to happen'?
- Why was it so unexpected, by markets, international agencies, and academic specialists?
- Why was Indonesia so much worse than the other countries?
- How should blame be apportioned among external and domestic factors, and among technical economic/financial factors and broader political and social variables?

The major argument in this section is that it was the conjunction of many factors which caused the crisis: political, social and economic; longer term and structural, and immediate and short-term; and domestic and international. It is also necessary — though empirically not easy — to distinguish between the factors leading up to the crisis, and the government's management of it. The former is concerned with a range of precipitating and vulnerability factors up to mid-1997, while the latter focuses on the domestic and international response once the crisis hit. If there had been no 'Thailand', and if Indonesia had not had to negotiate the complexities of a major political transition, as well as grapple with the economic-financial crisis, it is arguable that 1997–98 could have been a much less painless adjustment, perhaps not much more severe than that of 1985–86.

It is no exaggeration to state that in Indonesia practically *everything* went wrong at once over the period 1997–98. Some may find such a broad and eclectic approach rather frustrating — nothing satisfies more than a single grand theory! However, the pieces to the jig-saw puzzle comprise such disparate parts that I doubt whether such an approach will ever really work. Moreover, we need to acknowledge that, while modelling exercises provide important insights, especially in comprehending the recovery trajectories and quantifying the impacts of sudden changes in risk perceptions (McKibbin 1999), they are as yet unable to come up with integrated quantitative explanations.

Two years after the crisis, there is an emerging professional consensus on the key causes, which is also able to draw on the Latin American (especially Mexican) crises literature of the 1980s and 1990s. We can draw on this literature to look backwards at Indonesia over the immediate pre-crisis years, in an effort to sort out which variables were more and less important causal factors.

At least six broad sets of factors have been offered in the literature to explain crashes past and present. Some are contributors to a bigger story, others as principal or even exclusive explanations. We will sift through these theories shortly in looking at Indonesia in more detail.

First is the argument that international financial markets are inherently unstable, that they are prone to wild swings of sentiment, of boom ("bubbles") and bust, of euphoria and panic (Kindleberger 1989; Radelet and Sachs 1998). One characterization of the East Asian crisis economies is that "irrational exuberance" suddenly became "irrational pessimism". Such theories have been given credence by perhaps the most famous participant in these markets in the 1990s, George Soros

(1998), who described international capital flows as "a wrecker's ball".

A second, related school of thought links these explanations more explicitly to developments in international capital markets in the 1990s, which rendered these markets still more unstable. These developments include particularly aggressive "push" factors from OECD economies: low interest rates and rising savings in some of them induced funds to enter global markets. Capital flows to emerging markets rose dramatically during the 1990s, from about $9 billion annually in much of the 1980s, to over $240 billion immediately before the crisis.[15] An increasing proportion of these funds were of short maturity. As the two major economies of the world, US and Japanese monetary policy are seen as most pertinent to these arguments. Low US rates accelerated the outflows, while monetary tightening induces inward flows. In some quarters it is asserted that higher US interest rates were an early contributing factor to the Mexican and Thai financial crises of 1994 and 1997 respectively. The gap in the 1990s between Japan's interest rates and Southeast Asian deposit rates was such that it outweighed exchange rate risks as Japanese financial firms borrowed domestically in yen and onlent to these markets.

According to both these arguments, poor quality information flows and analytical capacity contribute significantly to market instability, as manifested in 'over-shooting' and 'herd' behaviour. In the words of one senior Central Banker (Grenville 1998, p. 11):

> For the most part, [investors'] knowledge was so superficial that it could be (and was) overwhelmed by the arrival of relatively small amounts of new information. More importantly, investors without their own knowledge-base simply followed the herd. In such a world, it is rational for any individual player to shift with the herd when new perceptions arrive. Whatever the fundamentals, when the herd is running, you run with it.

Here too Japanese banks are singled out by some for harsh criticism, with one leading crises analyst asserting that "... they have no idea what risk is, as demonstrated by the fact that they have lent money into every losing proposition of the past 15 years". (Dornbusch 1997, p. 23)

The third and fourth hypotheses switch the focus primarily to domestic factors. The third, drawing primarily on the experience of chronic Latin American crises of the 1970-1980s, attributes responsibility to macroeconomic policy weaknesses (Krugman 1979). In particular, there is a rigid nominal exchange rate combined with loose fiscal policy, the ensuing inflation from which results in an appreciating real effective exchange rate, a widening current account deficit, and capital flight in anticipation of — and eventually triggering — a balance of payments crisis.

Modern variants of this thesis include the argument that, while fiscal policy may superficially appear to be satisfactory, a conservative consolidated public sector account may conceal problems: even with a balanced budget, governments can waste resources; "headline" fiscal surpluses are easier to achieve during periods of sustained high economic growth; uneconomic/"crony" projects may simply be transferred off-budget to the banking sector through central bank credits or "command lending" to commercial banks; or there may exist implicit government guarantees which, if called in, could jeopardize fiscal balances.

Another variant is that it is possible to violate the Mundell-Fleming thesis (that governments cannot run an autonomous monetary policy in the presence of an open capital account and fixed exchange rate) if, as in the 1980s, domestic markets are only weakly integrated into the international market, capital flows take the form mainly of government borrowings and long-term FDI (and such private capital movements are small in magnitude). However, such a monetary stance is no longer possible with the highly mobile, interest-rate sensitive private capital flows of the 1990s.

The fourth hypothesis concerns the state of the domestic financial sector, and Krugman's memorable characterization of it being "over-guaranteed but under-regulated". Problems of moral hazard, occasioned by explicit or implicit government guarantees, induce reckless lending behaviour, especially to and by the politically well-connected. Prudential regulation and the legal infrastructure underpinning banks' operations are weak. Financial sector reports are not highly credible. The financial sector thrives in an environment of high growth, but serious shocks to the system may quickly erode confidence, and the herd behaviour discussed above could swiftly lead to a withdrawal of liquidity, bank runs and financial collapse. High and rapidly rising credit exposures by a shaky financial sector further complicate the problems of crisis management, since monetary policy tightening (for example in defence of a currency) imperil financial institutions. Moreover, currency and financial crises are conceptually separable, but in practice the two frequently go hand-in-hand, thus exacerbating the problem.

The fifth hypothesis (articulated for example by Hughes 1999) generalizes this argument to a critique of Asian-style "crony capitalism", corruption and poor governance — KKN (*korupsi, kolusi,* nepotism) in Indonesian parlance.[16] A variant of this so-called "Washington consensus" would add the absence of democracy to these fatal flaws. Apparently cautious macro-economic management and a partially liberalized economy can achieve impressive growth rates. These in turn are further bolstered by international development agencies, hopeful of continuing reforms and keen to develop their lending portfolios, and private capital inflows. However, it is argued, such a strategy conceals deeper problems. It does not deliver sustained growth, and it may well end up in crisis: the export sector begins to falter owing to the inefficiencies it has to carry; large uneconomic projects (selected on the basis of cronyism, or misguided hopes of picking winners, or both) do not provide a revenue flow sufficient to service debts; and an intricate web of vested interests prevents or frustrates the capacity of governments to act decisively in a crisis.

Finally there is the argument that international development agencies, in particular the IMF and to a lesser extent that World Bank and the Asian Development Bank, mishandled the early stages of the East Asian crisis and deepened it. The IMF was the critical agency in orchestrating the international rescue effort, since virtually all foreign aid was contingent on its stamp of approval.[17] These agencies, it is alleged, demanded tighter fiscal and monetary policy when budgets were broadly in balance, and when the economy was already beginning to contract. They attempted to resolve banking sector distress too quickly, thus aggravating the general loss of confidence. And they overloaded the reform agenda, forcing bureaucratically stretched and politically shaky governments to quickly tackle a vast array of highly complex and sensitive policy issues. From the middle of 1997, this IMF conditionality has largely been in the public domain, and is therefore amenable to public scrutiny. An additional concern, which cannot be tested, is that IMF advice pre-crisis was not sufficiently focused on core issues of financial and macroeconomic management, but was too 'scatter-gun' in its approach, and broached 'non-core' issues such as trade reform and state-sanctioned preferential trading and licensing privileges. These criticisms, it should obviously be noted, are not directed at explaining the onset of the crisis, but rather its prolonged severity.

How plausible are these arguments for Indonesia? Two additional points need to be emphasized at the outset. First, one of the key points to emerge from the crisis literature is the interactive effects of various vulnerability indicators, and the presence of thresholds beyond which a moderately serious crisis suddenly becomes very severe. In the words of Dornbusch (1997, p. 21): "Vulnerability means that if something goes wrong, then suddenly a lot goes wrong." Panic and volatile shifts in risk assessment, combined with unpredictable political developments, render attempts at definitive assessments of crisis episodes a hazardous exercise.

Secondly, it is necessary to distinguish between, and chart the interaction among, precipitating "triggers" and core "vulner-ability" factors. The trigger for East Asia's crisis was obviously Thailand. The Thai case is distinguished by the fact that there were clearly some early warning indicators — by early 1997, short term capital was flowing out and the stock market was declining.[18] Indonesia by comparison arguably had a foot in both camps: like Thailand it was vulnerable in some key areas, but it did not display the early signs of crisis in the first half of 1997. As the World Bank (1998*b*, pp. 54–5) argued: "It is clear that while a crisis was building quickly in Thailand, and to some extent in Korea, other countries — Malaysia, Indonesia and the Philippines — seem to have been affected by the crisis through contagion."

The proximate cause of Thailand's difficulties seems to have been a sharp slowdown in export growth in 1996, which quickly fuelled expectations of a currency depreciation. The prospect of tighter US monetary policy over this period may also have been a factor, as it attracted short term capital flows back into that country. Thailand was somewhat more vulnerable owing to its exceptionally large current account deficits. Declining bureaucratic quality and autonomy in key macroeconomic portfolios appears to have been a factor. Moreover, in the early 1990s, anxious to establish Bangkok as a regional financial centre in competition with Singapore and Hong Kong, the government opened the international capital account too quickly given the country's shaky financial foundations. Whatever the case, the market appeared to be convinced that a depreciation of the baht was imminent. The government resisted market sentiment for several months, in the process rapidly running down its international reserves, and precipitating on July 2 a bigger bang than would otherwise have been the case when it finally accepted the inevitable reality.

Indonesia-Thai merchandise trade connections are quite weak, and thus it is clear that the transmission mechanism for this contagion was the capital account. That is, events in Thailand triggered rising region-wide risk perceptions, and an ensuing flight of capital out of neighbours' currencies and countries, the more so in countries such as Indonesia with broadly similar economic structures and commercial climates.[19] (Conversely, it might also be argued that, after the onset of the crisis, financial markets became somewhat more discerning in assessing country risk, since during Indonesia's worst months of 1998 — January and May — there was no evidence of major 'reverse contagion' back to Thailand.)

The remainder of this section considers in turn each of the alternative crisis explanations for Indonesia, and then assesses their interaction with the management of the crisis from mid-1997 onwards. The analyses draws on a range of commonly used vulnerability indicators, some of which are summarized in Table 10 for Indonesia and its neighbours.[20]

Pre-Crisis Vulnerability Factors

(i) External debt and capital mobility
The first and second hypotheses may be considered together owing to substantial overlap. There can be no doubting the rapid build-up, and volatility, of private capital flows immediately prior to, and during the onset of, the East Asian crisis. For example, net inflows to the five most affected economies totalled $97.1 billion in 1996, whereas in 1997 there was a net outflow of $11.9 billion (World Bank 1998*b*, p. 10). As noted above (Table 5), the reversal was particularly acute in Indonesia, with net private capital inflows in FY 1996/97 (that is, in the year through to 31 March 1997) of $13.5 billion, followed by net outflows of $11.8 billion a year later (and an estimated additional outflow of $10.8 billion in 1998/99).

Of special note is the behaviour of the various components of the capital account. The switch in portfolio and debt flows was particularly pronounced: $90.8 billion inflow followed by $18.3 billion outflow. By contrast, aggregate foreign direct investment flows to the five economies were broadly constant in both years, at around $6.3 billion (with Indonesia as noted earlier the conspicuous exception), reflecting the importance of longer-term factors in the decision to invest.

To make the case that international capital markets were a problem, one has to focus on both national policies and the international environment, and the interaction between them. We examine below the domestic aspects, that is, the issue of

TABLE 10
Southeast Asia: Pre-Crisis Indicators
(all %, and for the years 1994–96, unless otherwise indicated)

Indicator	Ind	Mal	Phil	Sing	Thai	VN
GDS/GDP	25.0	40.2	17.3	50.6	35.4	17.2
Fiscal/GDP	0.2	1.3	0.7	13.1	1.9	–2.8
Inflation	8.1	3.5	8.6	2.1	5.4	10.5
CAD/GDP	2.8	6.9	4.0	+13.5	7.2	11.0
Debt/GDP	54	na	51	na	48	35
ST/Total debt	26	na	17	na	48	na
REER, 1996 (1990=100)	104	111	115	115	106	115
Internat reserves (months of imports)	6.0	4.7	4.0	7.1	5.7	2.1
ST debt/internat reserves, 1997	1.9	0.8	0.9	na	1.7	na
Euromoney rating (Sept 1996; 0–100)	71	80	62	96	77	52
Non-performing loans as % of total assets, 1997	12	8	6	2	15	na

Sources: Asia Pacific Economics Group, *Asia Pacific Profiles 1998* (Canberra, 1998); Asian Development Bank, *Asian Development Outlook 1998* (Manila, 1998); World Bank, *World Development Indicators 1997* (Washington D.C., 1997); JP Morgan for REERs (increase indicates appreciation).

whether an open capital account is desirable, and consider first the flows in aggregate, and whether there were signs that a problem was building up in Indonesia. In particular, the attention here is on the components of capital which are mobile in the short run (defined usually as less than one year). Depending on the measure used, it is possible to discern a potential crisis in the making.

First, Indonesia's external debt as a percentage of GDP was broadly stable pre-crisis, at approximately 54%. By the end of 1998, it totalled $142 billion, with the private sector owing slightly more than the public (Table 11). Pre-crisis the public debt to GDP ratio was declining, as indeed was the absolute total in some years, as a result of cautious fiscal policy and some pre-payments of existing debts (Table 12). Thus, for example, the share of public debt in total debt declined from 75% in 1991 to 60% in 1995 and 42% in 1997. If Indonesia's external debt is seen as being a key factor in the crisis, then this was very much a private sector phenomenon.

Much more problematic are the various estimates of short-term debt, and on this crucial variable we lack reliable time series data. The Bank Indonesia data on short-term debt (defined as one-year maturity or less) in Table 12 suggest, implausibly, that there was virtually no increase over the period 1991–95. It then doubled between 1995 and 1997. But this increase was almost entirely the result of the inclusion of previously neglected off-shore securities, for which data from previous years are not available. Alternative estimates of short-term debt suggest a much faster build-up. For example, according to the World Bank, *World Development Indicators*, it almost trebled 1990–96, from $11.1 billion (16% of the total) to $32.2 billion (25%).[21]

Although hardly at stratospheric levels, here was one significant early warning indicator. Indonesia's external debt was sizeable well before the crisis, much of it accumulated during the 1980s when it had successfully negotiated the collapse in oil prices. The rapid increase in private debt — particularly that (unknown) portion which could quickly leave the country — was a new phenomenon for Indonesia, and one which the government was not well-equipped to handle. In this respect, Indonesia differed from Singapore and Malaysia, with their more sophisticated, internationally integrated financial systems. One obvious implication of this rising short-term debt is that the conventional way of viewing international reserves was flawed. Instead of viewing the reserves in a current account context, in terms of months of imports, a capital account yardstick has become more

TABLE 11
Indonesia's External Debt, 1998
(US$ billions, 30 September)

Sector		Debt	
Public			68.6
Government		58.8	
SOEs		9.8	
banks	4.5		
corporations	5.3		
Private			73.3
Banks		6.5	
Corporations		66.8	
TOTAL			141.9
Memo items			
(a) Corporate debt composition:			72.1
SOEs		5.3	
Foreign-owned		31.9	
Domestic private firms		31.1	
Domestic securities		3.8	
(b) Banking sector composition:			11.0
State banks		4.4	
Private (foreign & domestic)		6.5	
Domestic securities		0.2	

Notes: Domestic securities are those owned by non-residents.
Source: Bank Indonesia.

relevant. As Table 10 demonstrates, estimates of the ratio of short-term debt to international reserves indicate that Indonesia was the most vulnerable in Southeast Asia, with a short-term debt almost double the level of reserves. Thailand was not far below, and was in turn about double these ratios of Malaysia and the Philippines.

Of course, what constitutes "mobile capital" is a matter of debate. External debt is only part of the story. Portfolio investment can also leave the country at short notice, and Indonesia received large quantities of this capital when the stock market was deregulated in late 1988. Adding the stock of portfolio investment to the short-term debt produces a still higher figure. Ultimately, almost all financial assets — foreign and domestic — might be regarded as internationally mobile if, as in Indonesia, there is an open capital account and there is a total loss of confidence in a regime. Indeed, crises invariably commence with *domestic* capital flight, since this group of investors generally has a superior understanding of domestic economics and politics. On this basis, the most appropriate ratio might be broad money (M2) to reserves. Alternative estimates (see, for example, Athukorala and Warr 1999 and World Bank 1998*b*) report broadly similar rankings, with Indonesia consistently among the more vulnerable economies both in terms of levels and rates of increase.[22]

Thus, in sum, there was a build-up in the stock of 'mobile capital', including short-term external debt and portfolio investment. But most of these indicators were not approaching crisis levels, and it would be a mistake to focus just on the foreign dimensions. More important, when a really deep crisis developed, was the stock of "liquid capital", as foreigners and residents alike took refuge from the rupiah.

(ii) Poor macroeconomic management

As was emphasized above, this was definitely not an old-style macroeconomic crisis (see Table 10). Indonesia had experienced nearly three decades of conventionally sound macroeconomic management. First, budget deficits were broadly in balance, had rarely exceeded 2% of GDP in any year, and were tending recently towards a modest surplus.[23] Secondly, inflation had been under control since the late 1960s. One of the proudest boasts of the Soeharto regime — justifiably — was its defeat of the rampant 1960s hyper-inflation. Since the mid 1980s inflation had always been at single-digit levels. Thirdly, there did not appear to be any serious exchange rate misalignment. The government had been basically targeting a constant Rupiah-$ rate in real terms (that is, with nominal depreciations of a magnitude similar to the two countries' inflation differential). Moreover, a policy of more flexible exchange rate management was being pursued, through a widening of the intervention band, as the Central Bank Governor over this period has emphasized (Soedradjad 1999). And on each occasion the band was widened — five times 1994–97 — the market pushed the rate to the bottom limit (i.e., the maximum possible appreciation).

However, while on the surface there appeared to be no looming crisis, here too problems were emerging. The principal one, à la Mundell-Fleming, was the attempt to set monetary policy targets and to run a quasi-fixed exchange rate with an open capital account, which facilitated rapidly rising capital inflows. A particular issue was the attempt to use one instrument (monetary policy) for two objectives, that is, one internal (inflation) and the other external (competitiveness). Through the 1990s the government resorted to tighter monetary policy to counteract perceptions of an over-heated economy. But the resultant higher interest rates actually attracted more capital inflows, which in turned fuelled a further monetary expansion (McLeod 1997). As long as capital inflows were modest, and took the form primarily of public sector borrowings and foreign direct investment, the fundamental flaw in this strategy was contained. But rising private flows of the 1990s, which were not amenable to any of the government's policy levers then in use, progressively undermined exchange rate and monetary policy settings.

Moreover, the government had maintained its real exchange rate target since the last major nominal depreciation of September 1986, and its evident commitment to this strategy — as in Thailand — convinced borrowers and creditors alike that there would be no deviation. As a result, only a small proportion (estimated to be less than 30%) of the country's private external debt was hedged. For most of the 1990s, the differential between rupiah and foreign currency lending rates was in the range

10–15 percentage points. Thus the attraction of foreign borrowings, supplied by international financial institutions only too
keen to participate in Indonesia's booming economy, was
irresistible. The gap in lending rates far outweighed the likely
modest depreciation of the rupiah. The government's quite
explicit exchange rate commitments and, especially for the well-
connected, bail-outs for troubled debtors underpinned the
massive unhedged borrowings. The magnitude of the problem
became quickly evident only when, in the face of large-scale
capital flight from August 1997, the government's commitment
to a targeted normal exchange rate collapsed.[24]

It might be argued, with the benefit of hindsight, that the
government could have averted these problems by hanging on
to the pre-crisis exchange rate at all costs.[25] This proposition
hardly appears tenable. The recent experience of Thailand had
emboldened the foreign exchange market to gamble against
governments trying to adhere to a fixed rate. Moreover, Indonesia
was actually more vulnerable than Thailand according to various
ratios of mobile capital to international reserves. Indeed, at the
time, the Indonesian government was praised by most observers
for quickly floating rather than supporting the rupiah.

Two final observations concerning Indonesia's pre-crisis
macroeconomic management are pertinent. First, the assertion
that the official fiscal figures in reality disguised major problems
turned out not to be correct. While there were various implicit
bail-outs, mainly via lax monetary policy in the nine months of
panic from September 1997, and while a portion of government
expenditures had always been misdirected (to cronies and
investments in uneconomic SOEs), fiscal policy in aggregate has
been under control throughout the crisis. In fact, if anything
the problem in 1998 was that the deficit was too small, as the
projected figure for FY 1998–99 was progressively wound back
from about 8.5% of GDP to about 4.5%, owing to under-
expenditure.

Secondly, there continues to be some conjecture over pre-
crisis trends in the real effective exchange rate (REER). The
data in Tables 6 and 10 convey the impression that there was no

serious exchange rate misalignment in Indonesia, and that its appreciation was less than its neighbours. However, it is no simple matter to measure the REER accurately. The figures in this table are based on nominal rates adjusted for differences in each country's consumer price index. A more accurate measure might use wholesale price indices, or a 'true' measure, calculated as the ratio of the price of a basket of tradable goods compared to that of non-tradables. Alternative series produce different numbers, both in magnitude and even trends.[26] In addition, one needs to compare these trends with comparable data for Indonesia's competitors, China, India and some Southeast Asian and Latin American economies. Nevertheless, no series of which I am aware points to Indonesia's misalignment being the most serious, in the sense of its real appreciation being the sharpest, among the crisis economies. This reinforces our conclusion that the real problem was the quasi-fixed rate, combined with the open capital account and large inflows of mobile capital.

Thus, in sum, Indonesia's macroeconomic policy settings pre-crisis were basically sound. The one major deficiency concerned the exchange rate. The problem was not so much whether or not there was serious exchange rate misalignment, but rather the attempt to run a fixed rate against a backdrop of large inflows of mobile capital.

(iii) Poor financial regulation

Poor financial regulation, political interference in commercial bank lending, premature and hasty financial liberalization and an open international capital account are widely regarded as key factors explaining East Asia's crisis. These were indeed central to Indonesia, but the story is complex and not amenable to some of the sweeping generalizations that have been offered over the past two years.

The first point to note is that some early warning indicators were present, but a full assessment pre-crisis was hampered by data deficiencies — some intentional, others reflecting bureaucratic weaknesses. Comparative estimates of the incidence of non-performing loans placed Indonesia somewhat higher than most of its neighbours (Table 10). However, they were below Thailand, and hardly in the precarious range. Moreover, Bank Indonesia data on non-performing (NPLs) and bad loans showed no obvious build-up of a problem. In fact, these ratios were actually reported to be trending downwards slightly.[27] The problems appeared to be more serious among the state banks, and not their dynamic new private sector competitors: in the four years pre-crisis, both ratios in the former were generally at least three times higher than the latter. Banks were known to be flouting prudential regulations,[28] but these deviations were seen in part as teething problems in managing a new and complex financial system. Finally, although there were frequent reports that the levels of technical expertise in many of the new post-1988 private sector entrants were rudimentary, most knowledgable academic observers with firsthand experience argued that standards of prudential regulation and financial skills were gradually improving.[29]

A second cautionary factor was that the external debt of Indonesia's commercial banks never reached the levels of most of its neighbours, partly owing to the restrictions placed on the activities of the still-large SOEs. As shown in Table 11 above, banks accounted for just 8% of the country's external debt. Most government and corporate borrowing abroad did not go through the country's banks. This factor explains why, in spite of the severity of the crisis, the estimated cost of Indonesia's bank restructuring and recapitalization (relative to GDP) is similar to that of Korea, Thailand or Malaysia (see Table 16 below).

A third reason for the presumption that Indonesia's financial sector was not in such bad shape is that the country did not appear to have experienced such a "bubble" in asset prices as Thailand in the mid 1990s, and Japan earlier in the decade. After Indonesia's major liberalization of 1988, stock market capitalization rose dramatically (Table 13), but this reflected primarily the proliferation of new listings. The market index fluctuated considerably, but by 1996 it was only 50% higher than that of 1990, a smaller increase than had occurred in Malaysia, the Philippines, or Thailand pre-crisis (or at least until late 1996

TABLE 12
Indonesia's External Debt, 1991–98
(US$ billions, year-end)

	1991	1992	1993	1994	1995	1996	1997	1998
Total	65.7	73.3	80.6	96.5	107.8	110.1	136.1	142.0
Medium-long term	56.5	65.0	71.8	88.8	98.4	98.8	117.3	128.4
govt	49.1	53.3	57.5	63.6	64.4	60.0	57.8	62.5
private	7.4	11.8	14.3	25.2	34.0	37.8	57.6	64.4
securities							2.0	1.5
Short-term	9.2	8.3	8.8	7.7	9.5	13.4	18.8	13.6
govt			0.1	0.1		0.1	0.1	
private	9.2	8.3	8.7	7.6	9.4	13.3	10.4	9.3
securities							8.3	4.2

Notes: Data refer to the stock of external debt in December of each year, except for 1998 when the month is September. Short-term is defined as one year maturity or less. Government includes state enterprises. Minor discrepancies occur owing to rounding; remaining (minor) errors occur in the original source.
Source: Bank Indonesia.

in the case of the latter). Other indicators report a broadly similar story. Urban, and particularly capital city, real estate prices are often viewed as a major 'bubble indicator'. The construction industry in Jakarta was growing very rapidly in the 1990s, as it was nation-wide, and since the onset of the crisis occupancy levels have been very low. However, CBD office rentals were increasing quite modestly in the mid 1990s (Figure 5).

A final indicator of reasonable financial health is that corporate commercial performance indicators generally appeared quite satisfactory (Table 14). Among publicly listed corporations for which internationally comparable data were available over the period 1994–96, the return on assets was strong, difficulties in servicing interest payments were quite rare, and debt-equity ratios were moderately cautious. On all these indicators, Indonesia was comparable to its Southeast Asian neighbours,

TABLE 13
Southeast Asian Stock Market Performance pre-Crisis

	Indonesia	Malaysia	Philippines	Thailand
(a) Market Capitalization				
(US$ millions, year-end)				
1988	253	23,318	4,280	8,811
1989	2,254	39,842	11,965	25,648
1990	8,081	48,611	5,927	23,896
1991	6,823	58,627	10,197	35,815
1992	12,038	94,004	13,794	58,259
1993	32,953	220,328	40,327	130,510
1994	47,241	199,276	55,519	131,479
1995	66,585	222,729	58,859	141,507
1996	91,016	307,179	80,649	99,828
1997	29,105	93,608	31,361	23,538
(b) Market Index	1982=100	1977=100	1985=100	1984=100
1988	305	357	842	387
1989	400	565	1,105	879
1990	418	506	652	613
1991	247	556	1,152	711
1992	274	644	1,256	893
1993	589	1,275	3,196	1,683
1994	470	971	2,786	1,360
1995	514	995	2,594	1,281
1996	637	1,238	3,171	832
1997	402	594	1,891	373

Source: IFC, *1998 Factbook*, Emerging Markets Data Base, Washington, 1998.

and much superior to Korea and Japan. There simply were no ominous trends in the published data. Various corporate and national debt rating exercises were below the figures for Malaysia and Singapore, as would be expected. But they were satisfactory, and mostly improving.

There were of course serious problems, many of which were discussed anecdotally in Indonesia, but which have only come to

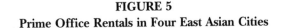

FIGURE 5
Prime Office Rentals in Four East Asian Cities

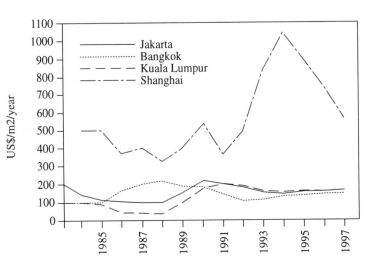

Source: Jones Lang Wootton, Research and Consultancy, as cited in Kenward
(1999).

light more comprehensively after the onset of the crisis. One
major, if obvious, point to emphasize is that financial data for
1997 and 1998 cannot be extrapolated backwards to prove that
there was a crisis in the making. The incidence of non-performing
loans and corporate insolvency rose dramatically because of the
collapse of the exchange rate (combined with the absence of
hedging) and the real sector. Banks experienced runs because
of a general loss of confidence in them from late 1997. Poor
commercial decisions in the euphoria of the pre-crisis boom of
course contributed to the problem. But many well-run and
professional banks and corporates were pulled down by these
economy-wide factors which were largely beyond their control
— a case of domestic contagion.

Seriously inadequate financial data, a weak regulatory and
legal framework, implicit government guarantees for the well-
connected, and the unwillingness (or inability) to implement

TABLE 14
Pre-Crisis Corporate Performance, 1994–97

Economy	Year	Sample	ROA	Not Repay	Debt-Equity
Indonesia	1994	258	5.5	0.8	2.0
	1995	275	5.1	1.2	2.1
	1996	268	4.4	1.8	1.9
	1997	14	4.1	3.7	2.3
Japan	1994	678	1.0	5.7	3.6
	1995	494	0.7	7.8	3.8
	1996	489	0.7	8.6	3.9
	1997	388	0.9	10.6	4.3
Korea	1994	224	1.9	5.2	4.7
	1995	226	1.5	5.8	5.4
	1996	81	0.4	10.9	6.2
	1997	29	–0.9	31.8	6.4
Malaysia	1994	592	6.8	2.1	1.2
	1995	653	6.4	4.6	1.6
	1996	695	5.9	5.0	1.9
	1997	374	5.2	5.3	2.2
Philippines	1994	110	4.5	3.6	1.6
	1995	138	5.0	5.9	1.5
	1996	140	4.4	6.5	1.6
	1997	49	4.7	7.9	1.9
Singapore	1994	289	5.5	4.6	1.5
	1995	298	3.9	5.1	1.8
	1996	310	3.8	4.6	2.0
	1997	113	4.5	6.1	2.1
Taiwan	1994	172	6.4	1.5	1.2
	1995	177	6.0	1.3	1.1
	1996	79	6.1	3.6	1.3
	1997	68	5.8	5.1	1.4
Thailand	1994	503	5.5	5.0	2.8
	1995	526	4.0	7.6	3.2
	1996	498	1.0	13.6	3.4
	1997	48	–13.1	34.8	4.1

Notes: The sample size refers to the number of reporting companies; ROA is the percentage return on assets; "Not Repay" refers to the share of firms which have interest expenses higher than their profits before interest, taxes and depreciation; the debt-equity figures are ratios.
Source: Claessens et al. (1998), based on Financial Times Extel data.

these regulations were of course present, and they did contribute to familiar moral hazard problems and the escalating crisis (Cole and Slade 1998). An open capital account exacerbated the problem, in the general manner described by McKinnon and Pill (1998), although it needs to be remembered again that the banks were not the major borrowers, and that a floating exchange rate might have overcome the particular problems associated with the open capital account. The financial market lacked depth and diversity (ironically in part owing to the government's fiscal caution, and the consequent absence of government bonds), and widespread insider trading continued to deter investors from the stock market, thus pushing investors into a narrow range of financial instruments.

In addition, domestic credit was expanding. Over the years 1991–96, the credit/GDP ratio grew at about 5% per annum in Indonesia and by 1996 it was about 0.5. This variable is frequently regarded in financial markets as an indicator of financial vulnerability, since high credit/GDP ratios weaken the capacity of central banks to push up interest rates in defence of the currency during a crisis. However, here too it was not obvious that there was a serious problem building up. Indonesia's ratio was growing more slowly than its neighbours, and just prior to the crisis it was less than half that of Thailand.[30]

Thus, in sum, Indonesia's financial sector was indeed "under-regulated and over-guaranteed" and these problems did contribute to the unfolding crisis. The "over-guaranteed" part of the equation was arguably more important, especially through its connection to the next causal factor to be examined, that of the Soeharto family businesses. Nevertheless, the evidence points to this factor as a contributing variable, rather than the key explanator. The pre-crisis data were admittedly quite inadequate, but Indonesia's financial vulnerability indicators (e.g., the ratio of outstanding bank credit to GDP) were only moderately high, and the financial sector was a relative small *direct* player in the country's external debt.

(iv) Corruption and governance

Finally, we consider the argument that widespread corruption and poor quality governance precipitated the crisis. This is a vast topic, and one which in most versions lacks an analytical framework. Moreover, it is probably more relevant to an understanding of the management of the crisis than to its causes.

It is empirically difficult to invoke corruption, which we use here as shorthand for the "KKN" phenomenon, as a key causal factor. The first problem is to demonstrate that corruption was extremely widespread in Soeharto's Indonesia. Obviously it was. But just how serious, and was it getting worse? Various estimates place Indonesia very high in comparative assessments. One widely quoted estimate, prepared annually by Transparency International, ranked Indonesia at 80 out of 85 countries in 1998. Most other surveys also clearly placed it towards the top. These exercises lack scientific rigour and are obviously highly subjective, but the story they tell is reasonably robust and probably quite accurate.[31]

There can be no doubting that the extraordinary concentration of power and privilege around Soeharto, and the dramatic expansion in his family's business empire, from a scale which was trivial in the 1970s and still quite modest in the mid-1980s. The expansion of his children's conglomerates was particularly remarkable. Nobody outside the family — or perhaps even in it — has a clear picture of the family fortune. According to one highly publicized estimate (*Time*, 24 May 1999), the figure may amount to about $15 billion. Backman (1999), in the most informative (if racy) recent account of the Soeharto family business empire, estimated that, at the time of resignation, Soeharto's family had significant shares in at least 1,251 companies. This figure includes the known holdings of the immediate Soeharto family, the spouses of his children, his grand-children, his half-brother Probosutedjo, and his cousin Sudwikatmono. Casting the net wider to a broader palace constellation would obviously result in a much larger figure. These holdings were spread over an extraordinarily diverse group of activities, including huge and widely publicized investments in satellites and telecommunications, toll roads, luxury hotels and tourism complexes, petrochemicals, an airline, shopping complexes, plantations, and mining.[32] Adam Schwarz's (1994, p. 136) assertion that "… hardly a single major infrastructure project has been awarded without one Soeharto relative or other having a piece of it", may have been overstated, but not greatly.

While the centralization of privilege and resources around Soeharto was undeniable, it is virtually impossible to reach any conclusion about aggregate trends in corruption, relative to the size of the economy, over the past couple of decades. One might even make a case — though it could never be proven — that the country was no more "corrupt" in 1997 than around 1980. In 1980, for example, the petroleum sector, state enterprises, and command lending at highly subsidized interest rates through the state banks were all far more sizeable, and these were massive sources of corruption.[33] In addition, Indonesia's trade regime had become far more open and less distorted by the mid 1990s following the major reforms which were initiated in the mid 1980s. There were fewer NTBs and the dispersion of tariff rates was lower (Fane and Condon 1996).

Whatever the case, these arguments do not demonstrate conclusively that corruption was a major causal variable. Other countries — China, India, Vietnam — also rank highly in these corruption comparisons but have not (yet) succumbed to the crisis. Moreover, one also has to explain how corrupt countries like Indonesia, and many others, could have grown so fast for so long with corruption an ever-present variable.[34] Finally, one needs to know a bit more about the type of corruption to make strong diagnoses. It matters a lot, for example, whether the proceeds of corruption go into Swiss bank accounts or are recycled into (admittedly high-cost) domestic investments.

Thus corruption was a serious problem, but it is difficult to advance the argument that it was a key precipitating variable. More plausible is the thesis that the particular forms corruption, and the political system in general, had assumed by the 1990s rendered the Soeharto government unwilling — indeed unable — to move decisively and swiftly once the crisis had hit. Our argument, to be developed shortly, is that corruption deserves great emphasis at this stage of the process, rather than as an initial precipitating factor.

Management of the Crisis

Thus far our examination of Indonesia pre-crisis suggests an economy moderately vulnerable to a crisis, but no more so than several of its neighbours. How, therefore, is one to explain the catastrophic events of 1997–98, which saw Indonesia plunge far more deeply? The explanation has to lie in the management of the crisis, which in turn was embedded in the fragile political system and escalating social and ethnic tensions. It is this to which we now turn. The major element of the story is domestic policy mismanagement which culminated in a total loss of confidence in the regime. This was compounded by an initially unhelpful international community, and coincidentally a range of additional adverse factors.

(i) A chronicle of policy errors

Chapter III above provided an overview of the course of the crisis, while Table 1 chronicled key economic and political events. As noted, initially Indonesia appeared to be handling the crisis effectively. Serious problems began to emerge by late October 1997, however, and the real damage was done over the next seven months, to May 1998. No economy could have been expected to have withstood the relentless battering which Indonesia experienced over this period. In retrospect these few months are the key to understanding how and why things went so bad so quickly.

The first major policy mistake was the sudden closure of 16 banks on 1 November 1997. This event was mishandled (by both the IMF and the Indonesian government) since it immediately undermined confidence in the entire financial system. The criteria for the closure of the banks were not well articulated, safeguards for depositors were not clear and were difficult to access, and there was no indication of whether other banks might also be closed without warning.[35] This event marked the beginning of a series of bank runs, and also the loss of monetary policy control as ever increasing amounts of liquidity were injected into the system to cover these runs.

The second set of problems related to the growing perception that President Soeharto was intent on protecting his family's commercial interests at all costs, a sentiment that quickly snowballed into a general loss of confidence in the regime's economic management credentials. The government began to backtrack almost immediately on the first IMF agreement (of 31 October 1997), particularly in protecting family business interests.[36] In early December Soeharto had serious health problems, and for a period was effectively incapacitated. In early January the annual budget was delivered, with key macro-economic assumptions which were hardly credible. Shortly afterwards, the rift with IMF became very public. With the presidential election just two months away, speculation intensified that the then Minister of State for Research and Technology, Dr B.J. Habibie, would become Vice President. When the rumours were effectively confirmed by Soeharto in the middle of the month, there was a further sharp loss of confidence, and the rupiah reached a new low. By then it was trading at just one-seventh of its pre-crisis dollar exchange rate.

The problems continued unabated. The government had just signed an impossibly ambitious agreement with the IMF. Indeed, shortly after the Soeharto-Camdessus high-profile, but controversial, signing ceremony (the controversy arising from the latter's personal bearing at the public event), Soeharto dismissed several of the conditions attached to it. In the following month, Soeharto toyed with the establishment of a currency board system, in the process dismissing his highly regarded central bank governor, and deepening the dispute with the IMF and bilateral donors. For a period, IMF support was suspended. The presidential and vice presidential elections proceeded according to script in March 1998, followed by the appointment of a contentious new cabinet, which included Soeharto's eldest daughter, Tutut, and one of his closest business cronies, the notorious Bob Hasan. For a brief period, the cabinet appeared as though it might be able to stop the rot, thanks mainly to the actions of a newly vigorous co-ordinating Economics Minister, Ginanjar Kartasasmita. But mounting political protests in May stymied these efforts, eventually tipping out Soeharto following persistent street protests and the loss of over 1,000 lives.

A third adverse factor over this period was that the inter-national community was initially rather unhelpful. This comment relates principally to the role of the IMF, an issue we address shortly.

The fourth point to observe over this critical period was that the crisis began to feed on itself. In addition to the mounting political uncertainty, the loss of monetary control contributed to rapidly increasing inflation and capital flight, and in consequence to the collapse of the rupiah. As shown above (Figure 4), the expansion of base money can be linked both directly to bank bail-outs (among which the well-connected were well-treated) and more generally to a sense of panic on the part of the monetary authorities. Monetary policy management was com-plicated not only by the financial and political crisis but also by the exchange rate crisis. Indonesian residents switched increasingly to foreign currency deposits (which are legal), thus complicating the task of money supply targeting. In this crucial respect, over this period Indonesia was without parallel among the crisis economies. Despite large currency depreciations, the other economies kept the money supply firmly under control, and inflation to single digit levels in both 1997 and 1998.

Finally, fiscal policy, as a counter-cyclical tool to help stimulate the economy, was slow to respond, for several reasons. Indonesia had a record of fiscal caution, and in the bureaucracy old habits die hard. The first IMF agreement compounded the problems, by stipulating a small fiscal surplus. There were also practical problems of how to finance the deficit. The Indonesian govern-ment does not formally issue bonds (although Central Bank Certificates, SBIs, amount to much the same thing). Perhaps the biggest obstacle of all was how, and on what, to spend any deliberately stimulatory fiscal measures. The crisis occurred against an increasingly volatile political backdrop. As the end of the Soeharto regime became imminent, allegations of KKN and attempts to settle old scores proliferated. In consequence, parts of the bureaucracy were effectively immobilized by the threat of public protests and accusation. Moreover, civil service morale was declining, the formerly well-defined lines of authority were becoming blurred, real salaries were falling precipitously, and the pressure was quickly intensifying for regional decentralization and even autonomy. Consequently, just at the very time that conventional Keynesian-style fiscal remedies were required in Indonesia (see Corden 1998), domestic and international factors conspired to remove this option for about nine crucial months. The IMF quickly changed its tune on this issue, during the first quarter of 1998, but throughout FY1998–99 the government progressively revised downwards its projected fiscal deficit.

Nevertheless, having made the case for the argument that fiscal policy should have been more, and more promptly, expansionary, this was not a major factor in the unfolding crisis. The financial, exchange rate and political crises were far more severe. At best, more government spending might have contributed to a marginally quicker economic recovery, and it could have helped alleviate some of the social hardship.

Having chronicled the major policy mistakes and lost opportunities in the first nine months of the crisis, let us look again more closely at the two major actors, the Soeharto regime and the IMF.

(ii) KKN again
If it is difficult to mount a case for corruption precipitating the crisis, the argument that it incapacitated the Soeharto regime once the crisis had hit is much more compelling. The distinguishing feature of the regime had been the immense and increasing power centred around Soeharto (MacIntyre 1999). "Soeharto in supreme control" was how Mackie and MacIntyre (1994) characterized the regime from 1982 onwards. In consequence, as noted above, corruption too became ever more centralized around the palace. Indeed, the public perception

was of the Soeharto children, together with a few key *pribumi* and ethnic Chinese business associates, enriching themselves grossly. This trend also had the effect of souring the political atmosphere, and eroding public support for the regime. All this was occurring at a time when Indonesia's body politic was better educated and informed than ever before, and aware of countries in the region and beyond democratizing and attempting to clean up.

Moreover, Indonesia's corruption differed critically from its neighbours, where spoils of office were shared around more widely, through changes of government (e.g., India, Korea, Thailand), a federal political structure (e.g., Malaysia), or within a ruling political party (e.g., China, Vietnam).[37] The nearest parallel to Soeharto's Indonesia of the 1990s is perhaps the Marcos administration in the Philippines from about the late 1970s. There were major differences between the two regimes, principally the fact that Philippine economic performance had been sluggish in the last five years of Marcos' rule, and disastrous in the last two. Nevertheless, the similarities in the events leading up to the removal from office of the two leaders are striking: increasing cronyism and corruption, decreasing influence of the technocrats, an increasingly restive populace, a more difficult international environment, and rising short-term debt.[38]

While corruption became more centralized, the influence of the technocrats was diminishing. The 1993 cabinet marked a watershed in this respect, for it ended the era of the so-called "Berkeley Mafia", the gifted economists who had guided economic policy since 1967. For a period after the announcement of this cabinet it appeared that the group's two "elder statesmen", Widjojo Nitisastro and Ali Wardhana, were not even to be maintained as informal advisers. (Subsequently they were.) For the first time under Soeharto, the Bappenas (planning) portfolio did not go to an economist. At the same time, a number of key Habibie allies (the so-called "technologs"), with views opposed to the technocrats' economic orthodoxy, were included in the cabinet.

At the onset of the crisis, the three key economists in this cabinet, while technically able and widely admired for their professionalism, were in various ways incapacitated. For example, the Finance Minister, Mar'ie Mohammad, continued to run tight fiscal policy. But he reportedly rarely conferred directly with Soeharto, nor did he communicate with the foreign financial press. To the author's knowledge, he never held a conference with this press, who were the principal means of connecting Indonesia to the world's financial centres, throughout the crisis. Lines of communication between Soeharto and the central bank governor, Soedradjad Djiwandono, broke down over the issue of a currency board, and the governor was dismissed (and was anyway reportedly on the point of resignation) shortly before his term expired, itself a highly unusual event in the Soeharto regime. Over this period, also, the Co-ordinating Economics Minister, Saleh Afiff, was occasionally quite ill and required hospitalization.

Thus, by historical accident, the key economics portfolios were weakened just when they were most needed.[39] The late 1980s financial liberalization urgently required comprehensive follow-up regulation and supervision, yet they were sidelined. In the post cold war environment, Indonesia could no longer assume its key western allies would automatically support it in times of crisis; it had to present its case on the international stage more forcefully. Rapidly increasing and highly mobile capital flows meant that the old macroeconomic policy framework needed to be modified. And, most of all, the late 1990s crisis demanded a strong team listened to by their leader. On all counts, the system failed to deliver.

Indonesia's political system rested so absolutely on this one supremely powerful individual that it quickly began to crumble when Soeharto himself faltered from late 1997 (MacIntyre 1999). There were no institutional checks on his authority, and conversely no safeguards in the event of his failure in a crisis. The political crisis which developed so suddenly over this period had its roots in the early stages of the foreign exchange and financial crisis, but its origins were much deeper, in the political and social problems, and they quickly drove the economic collapse to new lows.

That Indonesia's crisis was not inevitable can be inferred in part from a comparison of several major economic, political and institutional parameters during 1997–98 with those prevailing during the country's last major crisis, in 1985–86. Recall then that Indonesia's terms of trade fell precipitously, following the halving of international oil prices at that time. The country was, in one sense, still a "petroleum economy", with oil and gas contributing almost three-quarters of merchandise exports and two-thirds of government revenue. But, unlike the late 1990s, Indonesia did not then follow Mexico into crisis in the first half of the 1980s.

The two periods are not directly comparable — the international environment was very different, while one was a problem in the current account and the other in the capital account. But if one reflects on several of the key parameters it becomes much easier to understand why a crisis occurred on one occasion but not the other. Table 15 summarizes some of these domestic and international parameters. In 1985–86, Soeharto was in complete control, while the key technocrats were unified and had his ear. The state was powerful, and the range of powerful actors opposed to quick and decisive reform was very limited. The rural economy was buoyant, and constituted a larger share of the economy and workforce. It was thus able to act more effectively as a sort of 'shock-absorber' which ameliorated the painful effects of structural adjustment. The international parameters were also most favourable in the 1980s. Foreign debt was long-term, concessional, and in the main owed to a small number of creditors; the country's relations with international agencies (especially the World Bank) were very close, and East Asia was about to enter a decade of unparalleled growth and restructuring. On every one of these key parameters, the situation in 1997–98 was quite the reverse. It is an unanswerable counter-factual question, but it could well have been the case that if even two or three of these variables had been more favourable in 1997–98,

TABLE 15
Indonesia: 1985–86 and 1997 Compared

Variable	1985–86	1997
Soeharto	in complete control	end in sight, health worries
Technocrats	powerful, unified	much weaker, less united; Habibie factor
External debt	mainly state, LT, few creditors	large pte, ST, many creditors, unhedged
International donors	strongly supportive	deep & public divisions
International economy	Plaza Accord (9/85) massive E. Asia restructuring	subdued E. Asian growth; Japan in crisis
Vested interests opposed to clean reform	some (e.g., SOEs, emerging family), but limited	powerful, some Palace-based
Rural economy	buoyant, rice self-sufficiency achieved	declining rice output, serious fires & drought

then Indonesia would not today be engulfed in such a crisis.

It is in this sense that 'corruption' contributed decisively to Indonesia's crisis. It was not simply a matter of an insatiably greedy first family, but also a political system which had lost its capacity to act decisively in a crisis, and thereby lacked credibility in the eyes of both domestic and foreign investors. When Soeharto lost his legitimacy by late 1997, the whole system ground to a halt. Tragically, it took another five months, in which the economy continued to deteriorate rapidly, before widespread public protest broke the impasse and toppled Soeharto.

(iii) The role of the IMF

Should the IMF also be cast in the role of a villain? This is a large and complex issue, on which professional opinion divides sharply, and one on which inevitably outsiders cannot be fully informed. It would be a mistake to attribute primary responsibility to this institution, but equally one cannot escape the conclusion that it mishandled the situation. There is no evidence that it was any better (or worse) than anyone else in foreseeing the crisis. There may have been private warnings, but this cannot be verified. There is certainly not a hint of deep concern in the Fund's public statements.[40] The Fund's early approach to the problem also appeared to constitute mis-diagnosis. A one-size-fits-all prescription of a fiscal surplus was seemingly based on the premise of profligate public sectors and high inflation, neither of which was accurate. Nor was tight fiscal policy required, as arguably one might have advanced the case in Thailand, to compensate for an exceptionally large current account deficit. The sudden bank closures of 1 November 1997, which precipitated the general loss of confidence in the banking system, were certainly conducted under Fund tutelage, if not direction.

The Fund's reform programmes have been excessively ambitious and comprehensive, to the extent that it is doubtful that the government of any G7 country would be willing to sign on to them, let alone the government of a poor country in crisis.[41] Rather than focusing on the key variables required for the restoration of market confidence, a "scatter-gun" approach seems to have been adopted. The Fund seems to have taken the decision early on that this was the opportunity it had long been waiting for, to push through practically every conceivable item on its Indonesian reform agenda. Most of these — but not all, as we shall argue shortly — were highly desirable, it should be added, if implemented at the right time, and by a government able to deliver. But in the circumstances of late 1997 and early 1998, failure was inevitable: an over-loaded, weak and demoralized bureaucracy was not even remotely capable of implementing such an ambitious agenda; those reforms requiring fundamental legal and institutional change will take years to effectively implement (a point emphasized by Lindsey (1998) in the case of legal reforms). In such an environment, markets lose yet more confidence in a government's "failure to comply" with an agreement; stock and foreign exchange markets fall again, and the so-called "revolving-door syndrome" results in a new round of negotiations which have little better prospect of success.

Beyond the technicalities of its prescriptions other, admittedly somewhat peripheral, criticisms might be directed at the Fund. The unofficial, but widely circulated, briefing by a senior IMF official to the *Washington Post* newspaper in early January 1998 outlining the Fund's unhappiness with the Soeharto government tarnished the reputation of an organization which accords great emphasis to high standards of official conduct. And for a body which rapidly became deeply immersed in the intricacies of Indonesian economic policy making, in the early stages of the programme it displayed a curious naivety towards Indonesian politics. The famous signing ceremony has already been referred to. Fund officials were reportedly genuinely surprised that Soeharto began almost immediately to disown the second IMF agreement (of January 15) to his domestic audience.

Most of these criticisms apply to the IMF's approach during the first six months of the crisis, and as Corden (1998) puts it, the Fund is a "fast learner". It changed direction quickly on fiscal policy, which as noted was not anyway a major factor in the crisis. It relaxed its monetary policy stance, and Indonesia's negative real interest rates since early 1998 suggest that this policy, too, has not been overly restrictive.[42] (By contrast, in Thailand, the jury is still out on this issue.) Moreover, the fund could not be accused of foisting premature financial liberalization or an open capital account on Indonesia since these were already long in place pre-crisis (since 1988 and 1971 respectively).

One lesson from the crisis is that the IMF should have focused its attention much more on the core problems associated with the financial and foreign exchange collapse. This does not preclude wider forays into the realm of microeconomic reform. But priorities do matter, given the Fund has limited technical resources, and also a limited capacity to influence government policy. Ensuring a well functioning and regulated financial sector is overwhelmingly more important than efforts to dismantle a national clove monopoly or a national car programme, outrageous though the latter two interventions (both in support of Tommy Soeharto's business empire) were. In the Fund's major evaluation of its activities in Indonesia, Korea, and Thailand (Lane et al. 1999), "Governance and Competition Policy" gets two pages and the 'overload' thesis just one paragraph, in a 147-page report. Yet these programmes feature centrally, explicitly or implicitly, in the Indonesian programme. Until the signing of IMF III (10 April 1998) there was a cumulative total of 117 policy commitments, across the following areas: fiscal policy (17); monetary and banking policy (17); bank restructuring (24); foreign trade (16); investment and deregulation (15); privatization (13); social safety net (2); environment (6); other (7). Most of these were desirable in some short or long-run sense. But aside from the general problem of overload, some were either completely irrelevant to the crisis or quite mistaken. An example of the former was the requirement that a new environmental law be enacted, while a new competition law (enacted by Parliament in February 1999) certainly belongs in the latter category, as will be argued shortly.

Thus in sum various criticisms can reasonably be levelled at the IMF. The worst of these is that it aggravated problems early in the crisis, and that it has bequeathed an enduring legacy of excessively complex microeconomic and institutional reform. Throughout much of 1998 its pronouncements had much reduced credibility, as indicated by the fact that the signing of agreements II–IV had almost no reaction in financial and foreign exchange markets. There is still a lurking mistrust of the Fund in Indonesia, and elsewhere, that it is an agency run primarily for the benefit of its principal shareholders, with a micro-economic reform agenda attuned to the interests of major OECD economies. Nevertheless, as we have argued, it would be a mistake to cast the IMF as the major villain of the piece. Moreover, as will be argued in the next section, it will almost certainly be an important part of Indonesia's economic recovery.

(iv) Additional adverse factors

To complete this story of "everything going wrong at once", four additional factors should be mentioned. First, and most important, the regional economic environment was subdued. This is a major difference in the comparison between East Asia 1997–98 and Mexico 1994–95. One of the reasons Mexico bounced back so quickly was because of its deep commercial and strategic enmeshment with North America, whose economy was growing strongly, and because the US quickly mobilized massive bilateral and international support (Dornbusch et al. 1995). By contrast, the dominant economy in East Asia, Japan, was and still is in big trouble. Although a very generous aid donor, it has been in recession for more than half a decade, and several of its banks are teetering on the brink of insolvency.[43] There is more than one Asian economy in crisis, and Indonesia has plunged deeper than Mexico did. Moreover, although Japan's economic ties with developing East Asia are close, they are not as deep as the Mexican-North American connection.

A second problem was that the El Nino phenomenon had caused a very serious drought in Indonesia, resulting in declining food crop production of as much as 8% per capita in 1997–98, and necessitating the first large-scale rice imports in over a decade, just as the country was experiencing a balance of payments crisis. Rice prices and supplies have always been a sensitive political barometer in Indonesia, especially during election periods. Yet Bulog's (the food logistics agency) rice stocks more than halved in the second half of 1997, and by January 1998 were at historically low levels (of around 1 million metric tons). Rice traders, especially Sino Indonesians, were also said to be reluctant to hold normal stock levels, owing to fears that they would be accused of hoarding and their premises ransacked.[44] For a period in early 1998 traditional exporters began to hold off on supplies because Indonesian importers were unable to open credible letters of credit. Serious rice shortages were in prospect and, although the problem was largely overcome by the breaking of the drought and increased emergency international aid, this factor added to the general air of tension and uncertainty for several months.

Thirdly, international oil prices were at an historic low throughout the period, so there was an additional problem caused by declining terms of trade.

Finally, related partly to the political turbulence, and uniquely in East Asia, Indonesia's social fabric came under severe stress. The role of the small Chinese community, numbering about 3% of the population and controlling perhaps up to 40% of the economy, has always been a sensitive issue. The breakdown in civil order in May 1998, and the systematic attacks on this community, deeply traumatized many ethnic Chinese (Wanandi 1999). Some left the country temporarily or permanently. Many took their money out. It is an open question whether Indonesia may not have suffered a sizeable permanent loss of capital and entrepreneurial skills, which this community has historically supplied. Moreover, this community has provided such a crucial conduit to the international business community, and particularly investors from Singapore, Hong Kong and Taiwan, that these ethnic tensions contributed directly to Indonesia's tarnished international business reputation. Subsequent localized violence, with nasty religious or ethnic overtones, in Ambon, West Kalimantan, Aceh, and East Timor, further contributed to the perception that the central government could not guarantee stability and security, and that Indonesia may even be in danger of disintegrating.

A Summing Up

Thus there was a truly complex set of events, political, social and economic, domestic and international, of varying intensity present in Indonesia during 1997–98. A trigger set these events moving, the contagion was surprisingly swift and fierce. It exposed Indonesia's core vulnerabilities, particularly its unsustainable exchange rate regime, its large stock of external debt and mobile capital in the context of an open capital account, and its shaky financial system. Once these problems set up a crisis, the political system and social texture proved quite unable to respond effectively. In its last six months the Soeharto regime presided over a catastrophic decline from which it will take the country at least several years to recover. Indeed, it is hard to think of a regime which has presided over a quarter of a century of impressive socio-economic achievement ending so ignominiously. International factors contributed to all these problems, but this was first and foremost a domestic crisis in its origins and prosecution.

In this respect there are parallels with the 1994–95 Mexican crisis, where a combination of euphoria, domestic policy mistakes, political turbulence and social disaffection contributed quite suddenly to "… the almost complete loss in confidence in Mexico, its institutions and its leaders …" (Edwards 1998*a*, p. 25)

VI

THE WAY AHEAD

What of the short to medium run prospects? It is possible to identify at least three alternative scenarios for Indonesia over the next few years. These are:

- "Mexico": a quick return to positive growth, in which in retrospect 1997–98 recedes as a passing aberration.
- "Aquino": a "muddle through" period, which halts the economic decline and arguably lays the foundation for a more durable recovery, but in which political instability and lack of economic policy coherence deny the country a quick return to strong and sustained growth.
- "Burma": an awful scenario in which Indonesia closes itself off from the world, both politically and commercially, and which results in declining living standards, political brutality, and possibly ethnic and geographic fragmentation.

It is already clear that Indonesia will not be able to immediately replicate the Mexican record. Nor, fortunately, does the third scenario look all that likely. Mexico returned to positive growth within six quarters and it regained its pre-crisis per capita GDP (though not personal income) within nine quarters (see OECD 1998). As noted, the key to its recovery was exceptionally strong export growth (60% in volume terms in the first year after the crisis), and a swift Washington-orchestrated bail-out. Indonesia's crisis has been deeper, and its recovery almost certainly will be slower, notwithstanding the hopeful signs to emerge in the first quarter of 1999 (1.34% growth, quarter on quarter; growth of 1–2% and inflation of 10% projected for FY 1999/2000).

Something like the Aquino scenario appears much more likely. But political, social and economic factors are currently so fluid in Indonesia that it is impossible to make forecasts with any confidence. Instead, a more useful approach is to identify some of the major parameters which hold the key to recovery and which will determine how quickly Indonesia returns to positive economic growth. The purpose of this section is offer such a framework.[45]

We focus here on five areas of domestic economic policy which will be central to economic recovery. These in turn are predicated on a supportive international environment, and the evolution of a political system which is conducive to sound economic policy making. An assessment of these two sets of pre-conditions is beyond the scope of this essay, but it will be useful to highlight briefly some salient points which are pertinent to both.

The notion of a supportive international environment em-braces three critical variables: the growth of the global, and particularly East Asian, economy; unhindered access for Indonesia's exports; and continued generosity on the part of the international donor community, including an effective role for the IMF. On all three counts, it is unlikely that Indonesia will receive a major, unexpected boost. But equally there are probably no real disasters in store. World economic growth slowed to about 1.9% in 1998, and forecasts suggest a similar figure for 1999, notwithstanding continuing strong North American growth. The worst appears to be over in most of East Asia. Japan remains the big imponderable, and much depends on how quickly it is able to resolve its daunting financial problems.

It is probable that markets for Indonesian exports will remain reasonably open. In the Western Pacific, the momentum towards trade liberalization which built up over the past 15 years may slow. But backtracking appears most unlikely. Japan is now very open for most import categories, China is intent on gaining admission to the WTO, and several economies in the region are constrained by IMF programmes. In North America and Europe, there have been signs of a protectionist response to East Asia's now highly competitive exchange rates, much of it taking the form of anti-dumping actions. Thus far, however, and notwithstanding the bluster, there is no evidence of a widespread resort to protectionism, and one hopes that this will remain the case. It would be tragic if a Washington-instituted campaign to promote trade liberalization in East Asia, via the IMF, was met with a protectionist response. If, through greatly reduced capital flows, the world does not allow Indonesia to run a current account deficit, then inevitably the country's exports have to increase relative to its imports.

The international donor community remains critical during the recovery process. Private capital flows on any scale are unlikely to return quickly, and thus to ease the adjustment process during the transition official flows will have to fill the gap, especially in funding fiscal deficits. After a slow start, the international community has been reasonably generous. Japan in particular is by far the most important bilateral donor, and it has extended its bilateral programme despite hardship at home.[46] It will be important to maintain this aid effort for some time to come, beyond the point when distant donors, confronted with multiple demands from aid recipients in distress, might perceive that the immediate crisis is over.

The role of the IMF has been changing quickly since 1997. From its initial mis-diagnosis, it has begun to respond much more flexibly. (Some argue that its programme now runs the risk of being "too" flexible, to the point of lacking coherence.) Its Indonesian disbursements have been substantially "frontloaded", with a result that its aid flows are now tapering off. By March 1999, $8.9 billion of the $11.2 billion of committed funds had already been disbursed, although no doubt additional programmes will be devised. As Indonesia enters new and unchartered political waters, one could argue that the IMF programme could become even more important, as a kind of "policy anchor", which exerts a cautioning influence over the possible excesses of the country's new and inexperienced politicians. However, the Fund's influence, and possibly engagement, will in all likelihood taper off, as it has to deal with crises elsewhere, and as its financial clout diminishes. The challenge in these circumstances will be to ensure enhanced "national ownership" of its programme, so that the positive components are not discarded.

The second pre-condition relates to the capacity of the emerging political system to deliver effective economic policy-making. This will be critical not only as a direct spur to the recovery process, but also as a means of sustaining extraordinary aid flows, that is, by reassuring the international community that its support will not be squandered. It is as yet not clear what sort of economic policy will emerge, as Indonesia hopefully makes the transition to become the world's third largest democracy. All the major political actors have to adjust from the politics of opposition to that of government. Their policy statements are highly general and lack substance. None has yet articulated a clear economic policy manifesto. Already several features of this new political economy environment stand out:

- No one political leader or party is likely to have a clear parliamentary majority. Thus coalitions, in the running of parliament and in the election of the president, will be the order of the day.
- These coalitions are likely, at least initially and probably in the longer term, to be pragmatic, opportunistic, and personality-based.
- Independent of any coalition arrangements, parliament is likely to behave in an unpredictable and assertive fashion. (Conversely, it may be that, once passed, legislation will be more "legitimate" and receive wider community acceptance.)
- By contrast, the bureaucracy is likely to be much weaker than it was during the Soeharto era. It will also be much more subservient to the parliament in important respects, and it will be under sustained public scrutiny, not least from a reinvigorated press.

- It will take a long time for effective, independent and credible institutions to develop. This applies particularly to the legal system. Thus reform packages which emphasize primarily the making of new laws rather than their implementation will produce uncertain — and probably unintended — results.
- There will be great pressure for increased regional autonomy, so that a lot of the new policy debates — and possibly quite a bit of the power — will shift to the provinces.[47]

The new policy debates will in all likelihood shift to a range of micro, distributional issues, in which the broad macroeconomic parameters are broadly fixed. Thus debates which in the past focused on the "technocrats" versus the "nationalists" or "technologs" (always, it should be noted, a great over-simplification) will increasingly shift towards the allocation of resources between regions, ethnic groups, and classes of enterprises. Such approaches are already evident in the Indonesian polity: many of the new and influential political actors endorse — or at least accept — Indonesia's engagement with the international economy, and regard past industrial policy interventions as undesirable, owing to their assistance for the politically powerful.[48] To a surprising extent, therefore, they appear to be quite comfortable with orthodox notions such as a "level playing field", but emphasize instead that this philosophy needs to be accompanied by special assistance for disadvantaged groups of firms or individuals. Whether this leads to a genuine change of direction, or simply a new form of "KKN", remains to be seen. Whatever the case, economic recovery in Indonesia is likely to be considerably slower than in the other crisis economies, not only because its economy fell much more in 1998, but also because the country needs to forge new political and admin-istrative systems before it can proceed forward with purpose. This in retrospect was one of the key failures of the Soeharto regime — a failure to prepare the country for change.

Underlying these changing political parameters is the challenge of how to handle the Soeharto family. Unlike other long-term, authoritarian leaders (such as, notably, Marcos and

Mobutu), he has not fled the country, and apparently shows no inclination to do so. His presence will inevitably continue to divide the nation, not least owing to allegations that he commands resources on such a scale that his supporters are able to destabilize the political system, its institutions, and its processes. There is also mounting pressure for the state to sequester his assets, and to prosecute him for corruption. As in the case of Marcos, this is likely to be a long and tedious process, with low and uncertain pay-offs, and it would be unfortunate if the new government gets sidetracked by the politics of revenge. The definition of what exactly constitutes corruption is complex: for example, many of the special privileges granted to family members, from toll roads, to free company shares and the national car programme, were quite "legal", if outrageous. There is also the question of how widely the "family" is defined for the purposes of punitive action. Moreover, funds abroad invariably prove extremely difficult to track down, although international disclosure requirements are now much stricter than before, and there is now little inclination in the OECD countries to protect close allies from the old "Cold War" days.

Still, something needs to be done. As noted earlier, the market has already wiped out much of the family's domestic assets held in the stock market. One practical step which commends itself is that family members' outstanding debts to the state banking system be called in and, in the event of non-compliance, they then be subject to bankruptcy proceedings. Such proceedings have already begun on a very minor scale as they affect one son (Tommy), but they could easily and quickly be extended to the entire family.

Returning to the economic policy agenda, five key areas of policy challenge stand out. All involve a large and complex set of issues, and analysis of them needs to be undertaken within the parameters alluded to above. It is not possible to canvas these issues extensively in this essay, and it must obviously be emphasized that there are no simple solutions. But it will be useful to highlight some of the major issues.

Monetary and Exchange Rate Policy

Indonesia's new macroeconomic framework is precarious, but probably working as well as possible in the circumstances. Essentially the government has shifted from an awkward combination of a money supply target, loosely defined, and a nominal exchange rate anchor (keeping the real rate against the dollar approximately constant), to a tighter money supply targeting and a floating exchange rate (albeit with some central bank "smoothing" intervention). By April 1999, six months of low inflation had been achieved. Thus the looming fear of hyper-inflation, and with it a rise in entrenched inflationary expectations, has abated. The exchange rate seems to have settled in the range 7,000–10,000, despite very serious social disturbances in February and March 1999. There is now a good chance that Indonesia has locked in its current, very competitive exchange rate, to the great benefit of its export industries. (In view of Indonesia's disappointing export response during the crisis, relative to its neighbours, a high priority for government policy will now be to ensure that other barriers to export performance are removed.)

However, both these monetary and exchange rate variables could be easily derailed.[49] A sudden loss of international confidence in Indonesia's social stability, political system, or the government's capacity to manage the recovery, could see renewed capital flight, especially as trading on the foreign exchange market remains thin, and IMF support is winding down. As long as fiscal deficits are primarily foreign-financed, the money supply goals are more easily managed. But while a short-term Keynesian fiscal stimulus is surely justified over the difficult period 1998–99, beyond the immediate crisis period, if the new political system generates irresistible demands for government expenditure, this fragile monetary stability could easily be jeopardized. Moreover, the process of bank recapitalization, and financial reform more generally, has barely begun. Renewed bank runs, pressure from the politically powerful for preferential assistance, and the sheer cost of recapitalization could all lead to a blow-out in money supply, and hence renewed inflation.

There will continue to be a constant clamour for a more stable exchange rate and for partial closure of the international capital account. Key economics spokesmen for major political parties (for example, Megawati's PDI-P and Amien Rais' PAN) have already enunciated such views. These are of course different sides of the same coin, although popular economic debate in Indonesia often does not make the connection. The appeal of greater exchange rate stability in the wake of the turmoil since mid-1997 is understandably powerful. Similarly, one can readily understand the capital account argument: countries with restrictions have not been as devastated as Indonesia (e.g., China, India), there is the moderately successful Malaysian experiment nearby, and the intellectual argument for it is quite respectable. However, as we will argue below, while there may be a case for some curbs on the inflow of "hot" money in good times, in the current environment any attempt to impose capital barriers would almost certainly backfire.

There will also be pressure to reduce interest rates. The government needs to conduct a delicate balancing act in this respect, aiming for lower rates to encourage an investment revival, while recognizing that inflationary expectations and (most particularly) risk premia have not completely disappeared.[50] Nominal interest rates have fallen appreciably since September 1998, and with continuing low inflation they could well be back to something approaching pre-crisis levels by the end of 1999.

Fiscal Policy

Here the analytical options are more straightforward, but the devil is in the detail. There is a strong case for a short-run fiscal stimulus (see Corden [1998] for a clear statement of the principles). Private demand, especially investment, has collapsed, and thus a fiscal stimulus is necessary to avoid an even deeper contraction. The usual objections to deficit financing are not so important in the crisis context: a large proportion of the deficit is being financed by donors;[51] there is no danger of the deficit "crowding out" the private sector; and the markets are unlikely to see a deficit as a dangerous loss of fiscal discipline, providing the government presents it as a temporary measure and as part of an analytically robust framework (for which an IMF blessing makes a positive contribution). The temporary nature of the fiscal stimulus can be underlined by building in a sunset clause, either time-bound or predicated on the return to positive economic growth.

Complex practical matters do intrude immediately, however. Theory provides very little guidance on how large the deficit ought to be, whether for example it should be 8.5% of GDP (the earlier target for FY 1998–99), or half that figure (close to the actual outcome). In practice, as noted, the government has continued to underspend during the crisis. For example, the disbursement of social safety net (SSN) expenditure has proceeded very slowly: by December 1998, two-thirds through FY 1998–99, only 30% of the funds had been disbursed, although the pace was picking up. Several factors explain the delays, including inertia, the Department of Finance's in-built fiscal conservatism, the difficulty of quickly identifying suitable projects, bureaucrats' fear of corruption allegations in a new and highly politicized environment, and uncertainty regarding likely new regional autonomy arrangements.

The issue of how to spend the deficit is of secondary importance in the first instance, but it quickly becomes the dominant consideration, as the government needs to avoid programmes which lock it into future commitments. Labour-intensive, poverty amelioration programmes immediately commend themselves, and they have received high priority (see below). The pressure for greater regional autonomy can also be met in part through increased disbursements to sub-national tiers of government, although ideally one would want such expenditure to be placed in the context of a coherent plan for centre-regional fiscal relations, and for allocations not to exceed these tiers' short-run absorptive capacities. Perhaps most important of all will be resistance to the demands of the "new cronies", whether it be for subsidized credit, infrastructure expenditures, bank bail-outs and much else.

Banking Reform and Corporate Debt Restructuring

This is a critical area. A prompt resolution is required to enable capital inflows to resume and the financial system to function again. Otherwise, Indonesia risks experiencing a Latin American-style "lost decade" of low or negative growth. Debts need to be rescheduled and written down. The pain needs to be distributed among both creditors and debtors. Short-term financing — and hence the IMF — is an important part of this process, but it will help only if there is a clearly established policy framework. In its absence, such packages may do little more than finance further capital flight. There are clear lessons from the Mexican debt resolution experience in 1994–95, as contrasted with 1982: the importance of governments providing a framework for commercially negotiated workouts, for cleaning out the books, but then to the maximum extent possible keeping out of the minutiae of these workouts, which are essentially a problem for debtors and creditors to resolve. That is, in current parlance, creditors need to be "bailed in not bailed out". As Krugman (1997) succinctly puts it: "In the 1980s [in Mexico] the relationship between the debtors and creditors was politicized ... the result of [which] was paralysis."

Progress has been slow. Indonesia's external debt is very large, its bureaucracy and institutions are not well prepared for dealing with the problem, and the international financial community — both existing creditors and potential new buyers — are holding back pending clearly established rules of the game. Table 16 gives a rough idea of the magnitude of Indonesia's current crisis in comparative international perspective. On both criteria, it is one of the worst in modern history — much worse than Mexico in 1994–95, while problems in the OECD economies (excluding Korea) pale into insignificance. These figures are of course extremely approximate, and both series for Indonesia are now known to be under-estimates. Some sources, for example, indicate that the country's NPLs could be as high as 85%, and the financial recapitalization and workouts some 80% of GDP.

There have been few tangible signs of a quick resolution in Indonesia. Foreign investor interest remains negligible. It will almost certainly remain so until after the general and presidential

TABLE 16
Financial Crises Compared

	"Resolution costs" (% of GDP)	% NPLs
Indonesia	50	75
Korea	60	50
Malaysia	45	35
Thailand	45	55
Chile, 1981–85	41	16
Mexico, 1994–95	15	11
Brazil, 1994–96	10	9
US, 1984–91	7	4
Sweden, 1991–93	4	11
Japan, 1990s	3	16

Notes: Resolution costs are expressed as a percentage of GDP in 1998 for the four Asian economies, and in the restructuring period for the other countries; NPLs refer to non-performing loans (as a percentage of total loans, during the peak crisis period).

Source: Asian Wall Street Journal, 22 October 1998, quoting Barclays Capital and the IMF.

elections, and the composition of Indonesia's first post-Soeharto democratic government is clear, and until the serious social tensions and anti-Chinese sentiments abate. Preliminary balance of payments figures for the fourth quarter of 1998 suggest that there were still net private capital outflows. FDI flows for 1998 were negative, in sharp contrast to the other crisis economies (Table 7 above). Some mergers and acquisitions are beginning to take place: Heinz-ABC in food manufacturing, Standard Chartered/Bank Bali, Danareksa, and ANZ-Panin in finance, Mulia Industrindo in manufacturing, and some of the subsidiaries of the giant Astra and Salim groups). But in aggregate the amounts are still small. Also, by April 1999 capital inflows began to push the Jakarta Stock Exchange up sharply. The privatization programme was basically stalled until late 1998, and there is pressure for a sizeable portion of the proceeds to be handed over to co-operatives. However, activity did at least pick up in the second quarter of 1999. Little movement has taken place under the umbrella of INDRA, and its June 1999 deadline has now been pushed back.

The Bankruptcy Law was finally promulgated in late 1998, but thus far its operations have disappointed the financial community, in particular as its findings appear to consistently favour debtors over creditors. It is perhaps not surprising that progress has been slow, in view of the legal and procedural complexities involved, compounded by the fact that judges typically receive less than one-tenth the salary of commercial lawyers. But it is difficult to see how large-scale debt work-outs can be achieved in the absence of effective bankruptcy mechanisms.[52]

Similarly, the modern financial sector is operating at just a fraction of its pre-crisis scale. After missing an earlier target, the government finally announced in mid-March its plans for financial recapitalization. Under the current plan, the government will provide 80% of the funds for the recapitalization of sound banks (to be financed through the sale of specially designated bonds), while the banks themselves must provide the remaining 20%. The initiative was much delayed, and accompanied by concern that some of the selected banks owe their status as much to political connections as financial soundness. Funding remains an issue: the sale of the bonds; and the financing of the estimated Rp34 trillion "carrying cost" (interest payments) in FY 1999/2000, half each of which is to come directly from the budget and from the proceeds of SOE sales. This carrying cost estimate is especially sensitive to (and probably excessively ambitious in its assumptions about) interest rate trends and privatization proceeds. It is likely that, even with the continuing steady decline in nominal interest rates, the actual figure will be at least double, and possibly treble, the budget forecast. Earlier estimates of the cost of financial recapitalization, in the region of Rp300 trillion, now appear far too sanguine. The upper ceiling could be in excess of Rp500 trillion. In both cases, the danger remains great that additional government bail-outs will be necessary, thus jeopardizing fiscal policy targets and therefore the entire macroeconomic framework.

As noted above, an underlying concern continues to be Indonesia's deep financial enmeshment with Japan, and the fact that Japanese banks have very little room to manoeuvre owing to their own parlous position.

Microeconomic and Sectoral Reform

Microeconomic reform under the Habibie administration, and probably beyond, represents a case study in stark contrast. On the one hand, Indonesia has been moving steadily forward in achieving a cleaner and more transparent trade regime, and its external commitments — to the IMF, APEC and AFTA — will likely ensure no significant backtracking. Conversely, as in most countries, the sectors are typically the domain of more intense rent-seeking pressures: government projects have to be allocated, distributional considerations intrude, and line ministries are more vulnerable to capture.

Much of the debate now centres around the concept *ekonomi rakyat* (people's economy) which, under the active sponsorship of Minister Adi Sasono, entails support for small-medium enterprises and cooperatives. Implicitly, and sometimes explicitly, this translates into support for *pribumi* enterprises. Other strands in the emerging microeconomic reform agenda are broadly and notionally linked to the objectives of creating a more transparent and equitable commercial environment, in which patronage, KKN and alliances between conglomerates, bureaucrats and politicians are to be checked. These objectives and their implementation raise a large set of complex economic and political issues, and it is only possible to highlight them briefly. Four policy areas illustrate the dimensions of this complexity.

(i) *Ekonomi rakyat:* In principle, the goals here are laudable. SMEs have been the backbone of industrial success stories like Taiwan, and in Indonesia there is an unhealthy gap between the ethnic Chinese community and much of the 97% or so *pribumi* community. But are subsidized credits and co-operatives the best tools to tackle this problem? It seems unlikely:

- Indonesia already has some well-functioning small-scale credit schemes (e.g., Kupedes).
- SMEs are not the worst affected group of enterprises in the current crisis; large debt-laden conglomerates are generally in much worse shape.
- Notwithstanding their popular appeal in the country, there is little evidence that co-operatives have the capacity to function as effective business units.

These credit subsidies can be substantial — loans at 10%, when deposit rates are still in the range 30–40%. (The volume of term deposits has been increasing since the introduction of the credit schemes, though it may be unfair to draw any causal connection.) There is a very real danger that the subsidies are creating a new group of rent-seekers, just as Indonesia is trying desperately to get rid of the old groups. Meanwhile, government programmes which could really help the poor — such as public education and health — continue to be starved of resources. Moreover, the rich have always been generously treated by Indonesia's "flexible" tax system. There may ultimately be a case for some sort of Malaysian-style NEP, but the provision of equity-oriented public goods on a much wider scale would be much more effective. It is also very doubtful whether the quality of Indonesia's public administration could match that of Malaysia's in the implementation of such a scheme (see Mackie 1998).

(ii) *Property rights:* Co-operatives are also featuring prominently in new plans to develop the cash crop sector. Under a regulation drawn up in January 1999 by the Department of Forestry and Estates, private plantations above a certain size will be forced to progressively divest shares to co-operatives. It is still unclear how, how much, and how quickly this divestment process will take place. But already, and combined with the general breakdown in law and order in parts of the country, it is creating great insecurity. Sporadic attempts at arbitrary takeovers of plantations have been reported. Export growth is one of the keys to Indonesian recovery, and cash crops are critical to rural prosperity. It would be tragic indeed if their performance was throttled by this new decree. Of course, if the private plantations had acquired their land by unjust or illegal means, there is an obvious case for redress. But this consideration does not appear to be the primary focus of the decree.

This issue links back immediately and more broadly to the position of the Sino Indonesian business community, which feels deeply threatened by both institutionalized political pressures and random acts of personal violence. The government faces an extremely complex challenge here: a secure and confident Chinese business community is critical to the country's economic recovery, and for the signal it sends to international investors; but the grievances of an influential *pribumi* constituency cannot be ignored. The solutions will involve a combination of the symbolic and the practical, as adumbrated above. But there are no quick fixes and simple solutions.

(iii) *A Competition Commission:*   In February 1999, Parliament passed a law to establish a powerful Competition Commission. It is doubtful whether, at this juncture in Indonesia's history, such a commission is needed. An open trade regime can act as a check on monopolies in most cases. (Singapore has high levels of seller concentration, but one doesn't hear much discussion of a "monopoly problem" there.) Industrial concentration has been declining since the mid 1980s, especially if allowance is made for the rising levels of imports facilitated by the trade reforms (Bird 1999). Many of Indonesia's anti-competitive problems have been the direct result of government-sanctioned monopolies, in the form of protection for cronies and state-owned enterprises. (The latter, curiously, appear to be exempt from the law, as are co-operatives and small-medium enterprise.) It would have been far simpler to remove these distortions at their source, rather than to create a whole new, complex apparatus.

The Commission will divert high-level bureaucratic resources from more pressing tasks. It will also add to the cost of doing business in Indonesia, as firms resort to traditional techniques to circumvent complex or unenforceable regulations. No doubt it will further complicate life for the Chinese business community, since many in Indonesia think of the monopoly problem not in terms of the usual Western competitive framework, but rather as a problem of Chinese or foreign business control. No doubt, also, the Commission will prove to be a gold-mine for lawyers, especially as so many of the law's provisions remain opaque; e.g., "markets" and concepts such as "injurious to competition" are nowhere defined, nor is it clear whether exports and imports are to be taken into account in the calculations.

(iv) *Privatization:*   This area provides yet another example of the complex interaction between ethnic tension, local-level pressures in the new political environment, and bureaucratic inertia and resistance. Indonesia has a large, poorly performing SOE sector, but one which has been sustained by resentment at non-*pribumi* and foreign commercial dominance, and by the government's ambitious industrialization objectives. Privatization was a key item in the IMF programme. It is important as a means of raising efficiency, attracting foreign capital, and bolstering the government's short-term fiscal position. However, progress was initially very slow. In FY 1998–99, the government projected assets sales of $1.5 billion, but actual receipts were less than one-third of this figure. The first SOE targeted for partial privatization, the cement company Semen Gresik, encountered serious and protracted local opposition, and ultimately the government's objective of 51% disposal was watered down to 14%, with the later possibility that the buyer (Mexico's Cemex) could increase its share. Then, just prior to the completion of the financial year, a 51% stake in the Jakarta International Container Terminal was sold to Hong Kong interests for $243 million. As the regional economic outlook improved, and the government became more experienced in SOE disposal, the pace has accelerated. In the first six weeks of the current FY, asset sales of $880 million were recorded, involving the Jakarta and Surabaya container point operators (51% and 49% shares respectively), and small shares of Salim's Indofood (which had been ceded to the government in payment for debts owed to the central bank) and the state-owned Telekomunikasi Indonesia. Several other SOEs are targeted for privatization in FY 1999/2000, including the country's international telephone company, the Jakarta airport manager, and mining and plantation companies. But the political pressures opposed to reform should not be underestimated.

Social Policy

This is an important component of the reform package, as a means of ameliorating the impact of the crisis on the poor and vulnerable, and maintaining societal cohesion during hard times and unprecedented socio-economic adjustment. These social safety net (SSN) measures are no substitute for economic recovery, but for particular groups and individuals they can make a difference.

The difficulties of devising and implementing SSN pro-grammes should not be under-estimated. First, the affected groups need to be identified, both in aggregate and by location. This is no simple matter. As shown above, the estimates of poverty incidence vary greatly. If, for example, the ILO estimates of 50% or more of the population in poverty were correct — which they almost certainly are not — then the appropriate response would simply be to aim for across-the-board subsidies of a few key items with high weights in the consumption bundles of the poor. Targeted social programmes can rarely fine-tune at a rate which is better than this, especially given Indonesia's bureaucratic capacities. If, as we now know, poverty incidence is much lower, the case for targeting is much stronger. But it is still no simple matter to identify regions, much less families and individuals, with serious social problems. Officials still have to work off old (i.e., pre-crisis) data bases in identifying poor localities, and there is much "turnover" in the composition of those below the poverty line.

Second, it is not obvious which programmes are the most cost-effective and quick-impacting. The government has adopted four main approaches: food security, including subsidies (the latter also extends to non-food items such as fuel); labour-intensive public works; social protection, including enhanced access to basic education and health services; and promotion of the *ekonomi rakyat*, especially co-operatives and SMEs.

Each of these approaches has strengths and weaknesses. Subsidies are a blunt instrument, which may encourage corruption, including export smuggling. If there are price controls, they act as a production disincentive for farmers; if budget support is used, then there is concern about fiscal sustainability, and possibly the adverse effects of inflation on the poor. Conversely, for very poor groups, cheap food may be the only short-run palliative measure. And it may be possible to fine tune these subsidies, by selecting certain food items not normally consumed by better off groups.[53]

Public works programmes have a record of quite successful implementation in Indonesia, having been initiated in the early Soeharto era as a means of quickly recycling the windfall oil revenues into rural areas (de Wit 1973). Thus there is a policy and administrative framework already in place. These programmes can also be used as a de facto regional policy tool, by giving special emphasis to poorer regions especially hurt by the crisis. Wage rates might be set at a level just below market rates in order to induce mainly the poor to take up the employment opportunities. However, the challenges in devising and implementing such programmes are significant. A formula for regional (provincial and sub-provincial) allocation of funds has to be established: it is not obvious that the current formulae are the most suitable, or that the government has the necessary socio-economic data to inform the decision-making process. Moreover, these programmes have to be implemented against a backdrop of escalating demands for decentralization, where lines of authority and responsibility are blurring. Finally, while the principal short-term focus has to be job creation, with little regard for the nature of the projects selected, beyond the very short-term, the quality of the investment is of concern, and the checks and balances in place to guard against both "KKN" and unwise investments are not always in place. Initial reports suggest that some of these programmes have been beset by serious corruption problems.

Social protection measures can help to cushion the impact of the crisis on the poor, while also helping to preserve the nation's human capital base. To the extent that poor families can be easily identified, fee waivers might encourage parents not to withdraw their children from school. Much depends here on what happens to the plethora of informal levies, which are typically much greater than the formal fees. Public health and family planning services need to be maintained wherever possible during the crisis, and there may also be a case for temporary subsidies for key pharmaceuticals, the prices of which have risen sharply. Perhaps unexpectedly, in view of the range of potential obstacles, these social protection programmes are thought to be working quite well. In the case of the scholarship schemes, for example, local educational authorities are presumably well placed to identify those in need, and there is also pressure on these officials to disburse the funds cleanly.

The measures to support the *ekonomi rakyat* are the most controversial, perhaps attracting the greatest political support but lacking a coherent economic rationale. The funds involved are very large (Manning, 1999): in FY 1999/2000 Rp20 trillion has been allocated to such programmes, equivalent to almost 10% of the entire budget and double that of the oil subsidy. As argued above, there is little evidence that credit and other subsidies for co-operatives and SMEs will have any significant anti-poverty impacts, although of course individual recipients of such largesse will benefit. There is a real danger of these programmes quickly degenerating into corrupt, politicized handouts, and of the government becoming locked into con-tinuing subsidies post-crisis. Moreover, although the schemes have a strong *pribumi* focus, it is tragically evident in West Kalimantan, Ambon, and elsewhere that social discord in Indonesia is much more than just the *pribumi*/ non-*pribumi* issue.

Conversely, proponents of these schemes point out, not without merit, that to the extent they can diffuse resentment at Sino-Indonesian commercial dominance, they may have some merit.

Finally, implementation is everywhere a major concern. The bureaucracy is under-resourced, demoralized, and suddenly politicized. Sub-national tiers of government want more resources and control. Government agencies are now adopting an extremely cautious approach to any new initiative, simply on the grounds that they may be subject to KKN allegations. There is pressure, both domestic and international, to engage NGOs in these new programmes. While such an approach is superficially attractive, and some cases would be preferable, these institutions vary enormously in quality and administrative capacity. Their involvement could just as easily compound the problems as resolve them.

*   *   *

Thus, in sum, Indonesia presents a very mixed picture since the removal of Soeharto. Its economic recovery has been, and will likely continue to be, much slower than that in the other crisis economies, and the political situation more unpredictable. On key policy issues, the government has — perhaps understandably — moved rather slowly. The macroeconomic policy framework appears to be bedded down, although it is precarious. Microeconomic policy could have been a lot worse, even though it is messy in parts. Perhaps of most concern, the politics of populism and newly emerging *pribumi* business interests threaten to sour the business environment. Banking recapitalization and debt work-outs are moving very slowly, but at least there are the beginnings of progress. Social programmes present a mixed picture, with some schemes apparently working well, and others marred by corruption.

It is most unlikely that Indonesia will return quickly to its pre-crisis high-growth trajectory. But there are glimmers of hope. Providing that (a) the macroeconomic framework holds together, (b) a reasonably open trade regime is adhered to, (c) a measure of political stability and social harmony is restored, and (d) the international outlook remains reasonably supportive, the country's highly competitive exchange rate can be expected to gradually deliver a capital-efficient (i.e., low ICOR), export-led recovery which will percolate through to the rest of the economy. The capital stock which has been built up over the last 20 years of very high investment levels is still intact, although over time it will depreciate. Indonesia's broadly-based and (still) resource-rich economy provides the basis for a diversified recovery in uncertain times. Neither the magnitude of the exodus of the ethnic Chinese community, nor (save for a handful) this group's alternative international business options, should be over-stated. And luck, a commodity conspicuously absent in Indonesia during most of the crisis, may finally be turning around, with good rains from mid-1998 and rising petroleum prices from March 1999.

More generally, although Indonesia's political parameters will probably remain uncertain for some time to come, none of its key political actors is fundamentally opposed to an open and liberal economy. Countries as diverse as Thailand and Italy have demonstrated that good macroeconomic fundamentals can still continue to generate quite strong growth, notwithstanding such seemingly formidable political obstacles. Consequently, while the immediate challenges are daunting, it would be a mistake just yet to consign Indonesia again to the "chronic dropout" category.

VII

BROADER ANALYTICAL ISSUES

Beyond the short-run considerations, major events such as these demand a reconsideration of the big policy framework, in an effort to avoid the recurrence of painful and traumatic episodes. As Garnaut (1998, p. 10) has argued:

> The shock of 1997 is a defining event in the economic history of East Asia. Like the Great Depression in the West, it has the capacity to change thought about economic development and economic policy in fundamental ways.

This is a vast topic which is beyond the immediate scope of this paper, but it might be useful to conclude with some observations on three key inter-related issues, capital controls, exchange rate policy and financial liberalization and supervision, particularly as they relate to Indonesia. The crisis has prompted a re-examination of many other issues, including arguments for co-ordinated international action to monitor and perhaps regulate short-term capital flows, the need for institutional reform, for greater attention to equity issues, and for a more skeptical view of the efficacy of industry policy. However, there are space constraints, and it makes sense for Indonesian policy-makers to focus first and foremost on the key domestic macroeconomic and financial challenges. In this context, these three are so centrally linked to recent events that they warrant the highest priority. The international community may one day be able to introduce a global regulatory environment which helps countries manage exogenous capital account shocks, but such a possibility is at best a small hope on the distant horizon.

Capital Controls (and Sequencing)?

Since the panic in financial markets triggered the sudden exodus of capital, and such great hardship for many, it is tempting to advocate the partial closure of the capital account, at least to the extent of controlling the movement of "hot money". India, China, and Vietnam, among others, have not experienced a crisis of the magnitude of Indonesia and Thailand, it is argued. Yet, apart from maintaining capital controls, their domestic policy settings were quite similar — quasi fixed exchange rates, very weak banking sectors, inefficient state enterprises, and plenty of corruption. The key problem, according to this view, is an open capital account — which has been the case in Indonesia since 1970, and increasingly so in Thailand during the 1990s. Furthermore, it is argued, capital flows are now of such magnitude that they can overwhelm even a well-managed domestic policy framework. For example, it is estimated that financial institutions globally manage about $20 trillion of funds. Most of these funds remain in their country of origin, and may not ever be globally mobile. But even a very small change in risk perceptions, for example leading to 0.1% increase in flows to a particular country, would hypothetically mean that it could receive funds of $20 billion, with major implications for the management of its monetary policy and exchange rate.

In effect, this argument is a variant of the sequencing literature, revisited (McKinnon 1993): the capital account should eventually be opened, but not until fiscal balance has been firmly set in place and domestic financial institutions are able to cope with international financial integration.

Malaysia's decision on 1 September 1998 to restrict short-term capital movements and peg the ringgit has added new impetus to these arguments. The case for capital controls has been strengthened empirically by the evidence from Chile which, after a financial crisis in the early 1980s resembling Southeast

Asia's experience in 1997/98 (though in aggregate not as severe — see Table 16), instituted major reforms of its banking system. In 1991, as private capital surged into the country, some restrictions on capital mobility were instituted to prevent significant asset price and exchange rate appreciation.[54] The fact that Chile survived both the Mexican and East Asian crises lends considerable support to the case for these controls.[55]

The case for capital controls is also attracting much intellectual support, and not just from those who are ideologically predisposed towards such regulation. A recent paper by Jagdish Bhagwati (1998), whose liberal trade credentials are beyond dispute, has set out forcefully the case for controls. He argues inter alia:

> Each time a crisis related to capital flows hits a country, it typically goes through the wringer. The debt crisis of the 1980s cost South America a decade of growth. (p. 8)

> ... the claims of enormous benefits from free capital mobility are not persuasive. Substantial gains have been asserted, not demonstrated, and most of the payoff can be obtained by direct equity investment. (p. 7)

> ... [debtor countries"] independence is lost not only directly to foreign nations but to an IMF increasingly extending its agenda, at the behest of the US Congress, to invade domestic policies on matters of social policy ... (p. 9)

The puzzling issue here is how Indonesia was able to operate so effectively with a completely open capital account for so long. Many observers, myself included, saw an open capital account as one of the building blocks of the country's macroeconomic success. We were persuaded by Professor Sumitro (see endnote 56) and others that controls would almost certainly break down in the face of corruption, especially with Singapore on the doorstep. It also seemed as though an open capital would, in a self-correcting manner, constitute a check on government excesses, as serious policy mistakes would trigger capital flight.

In retrospect, these checking mechanisms worked as long as short-term capital flows were not overwhelming, and as long as there were no really catastrophic political and economic problems. In other words, both pre-conditions for the strategy's success had effectively disappeared by the mid 1990s.

While the case for some short-term capital controls in a poorly regulated and corrupt financial sector is quite persuasive, it is hardly relevant to Indonesia's short-run recovery agenda. The immediate problem is encouraging the funds which have fled since late 1997 to return. When confidence in a country has reached an all-time low, any measure which renders the investment climate even less attractive would almost certainly be counter-productive. Advocating capital account closure now is akin to shutting the gate after the horse has bolted.

Moreover, proponents of the controls for Indonesia also have to come to grips with the issue of administrative feasibility, and the need to ensure that they are not seen as a substitute for more far-reaching reform of institutions, especially the banking sector. In the longer term, there may well be a case for some modest, transparent, ex ante, market-based constraints on the inflow of highly volatile and speculative short-term capital. It also needs to be emphasized that the policy options are not quite as black-and-white — "to control or not to control" — as is sometimes portrayed. Devising the modalities of such a scheme is one of the big policy challenges of our time. However, one must continue to worry about the feasibility of such controls in Indonesia. If the central bank and finance ministry cannot adequately supervise the financial sector, can they really be trusted to administer efficiently, fairly and without corruption a system of even moderate controls in a regional environment of porous international goods and capital markets? The "cure" could end up being far worse than the "disease".[56]

What Sort of Exchange Rate Policy?

The crisis has also prompted a rethink of exchange rate policy in Southeast Asia. Several countries in the region — again

Indonesia most prominently — seemed to defy Mundell-Fleming for a long time. That is, they were apparently able to run an autonomous monetary policy, and maintain a fixed exchange rate, in the context of an open capital account. The strategy of "fixed but flexible" exchange rates seemed to work well in the region, to the point where pragmatic considerations suggested that there was no reason to change.

Here also the crisis has taught us a lesson (Garnaut 1999). Countries essentially face the choice of a fixed exchange rate in the form of some sort of currency board arrangement, a fixed but adjustable exchange rate, or a freely floating regime. Within each alternative, there are of course variants, and the second and third can generate a hybrid option in the form of a heavily managed "float". The problem with the second option, which over the past two decades has been the preferred approach in Southeast Asia, is that it breaks down in the presence of large and volatile capital movements. Governments in the region had convinced themselves — and most importantly the financial markets — that they could continue to set and maintain the rate, to the point where few borrowers bothered to take out insurance against a depreciation. But, as we have seen, the strategy came unstuck in 1997, and as currencies crashed the regime was one of the key explanations for the unfolding crisis. Thus, for the crisis economies, such an option now looks much less attractive. That is, unless governments are also prepared to follow Malaysia in substantially restricting short-term capital movements; but this strategy creates other difficulties and is unlikely to be feasible in Indonesia in the foreseeable future.

What of the other options? In a well-managed macro-economy with financial depth, the general consensus of professional opinion would favour a floating regime, perhaps with some government intervention to smooth short-run fluctuations. Borrowers and traders can avail of financial instruments to hedge against uncertainty. Moreover, in the short-run, two of Southeast Asia's crisis economies are constrained by the IMF straitjacket, and they currently have little choice other than to go along with this option.

However, the floating regime has some drawbacks. In a jittery commercial environment in which government policy lacks credibility, it could lead to sharply oscillating exchange rates. The prospect of such fluctuations could attract currency speculators, thus compounding the problem. If financial markets are under-developed, and the uncertainty very great, it may be very difficult to take out hedging options. Governments may be tempted to over-do "smoothing" interventions and attempt to gamble against the market.

In these circumstances, some sort of currency board (CB) option again becomes worthy of consideration. CBs have attracted considerably notoriety in Southeast Asia in 1998, when in February then President Soeharto invited a prominent academic proponent of CBs, Stephen Hanke, to be his special adviser on the subject. The pros and cons of CBs then got drowned in controversy: the IMF objected that a CB was not in the framework agreement, the Bank Indonesia governor reportedly was dismissed (or resigned) in part owing to his opposition to the CB proposal, and the market plunged further in response to the stark policy disunity.

As long as Indonesia remains within the IMF framework, and the Fund itself opposes the scheme, a CB is not a realistic option in the immediate future. But the intellectual case for a CB is not without merit, especially for economies deep in crisis. The boards have a good track record. Hong Kong is the obvious case of success in East Asia, where one has been in operation since 1982, and where it seems to have succeeded in reassuring then fragile markets. In Argentina it brought inflation down dramatically, as it has in several other crisis and transition economies. It may seem preposterous to include Southeast Asia in such a group, Hong Kong excluded. But for Indonesia, at least, it is arguably the only serious option if the political leadership demands a fixed rate, providing the IMF can be persuaded to change its thinking.

It goes without saying, of course, that a CB would be no simple cure for Indonesia, and complex policy questions remain even if the IMF were to acquiesce. This was a principal objection by many Indonesian economists to the proposal: it was seized upon by Soeharto as some kind of "quick fix" cure, maybe also as a bargaining chip in his dealings with the IMF. (Some critics also allege that the proposal was attractive to his family, as it would have provided a means of taking their liquid assets abroad — to a safe haven — at a more favourable exchange rate.) There is the question of what rate to set the currency, and which currency anchor to choose. Policy makers and the community would have to fully understand, and accept, the loss of monetary policy independence implicit in the adoption of a CB. Currency uncertainty would be transmitted not via exchange rate, but interest rate, fluctuations. Especially in the transition phase, interest rates could go very high, with negative repercussions for the real economy. Nominal prices (including wages) would have to be completely flexible, for the fixed rate effectively introduces a major price rigidity into the system. This would be an especially important requirement in a commodity economy like Indonesia, which is subject to large movements in its terms of trade.[57] Above all else, there would have to be complete government commitment to running a pure and non-political CB: if the markets perceived that such a commitment was not present, as probably would have been the case under Soeharto, a massive liquidity drain would have pushed interest rates up so high, and for so long, as to destroy much of the real economy.

Financial Reform and Regulation

Financial reform and regulation lie at the heart of the Southeast Asian crisis, and are also central to its resolution. During the heady growth from the mid 1980s, the importance of a carefully managed financial system in underpinning this growth was overlooked. The assumption was that cautious fiscal policy, low inflation, high domestic savings rates, increasing financial depth and sophistication, and stronger international commercial engagement would help avoid a major financial disaster. This belief was further strengthened by the management of periodic minor financial stresses without undue difficulty in several of the countries.

With the benefit of hindsight it is clear that the policy regimes in Indonesia and Thailand were quite unable to adjust to the massive financial flows of the 1990s, in the context of fixed exchange rates, and poorly regulated, politicized financial systems. In both these economies financial liberalization occurred prematurely, in the sense that the opening up of the financial system was not accompanied by appropriate regulatory mechanisms.

Indonesia's major financial deregulations occurred in 1983 and 1988. Until the October 1988 ("Pakto") reforms, there was an extremely inefficient, state-dominated banking sector, which generally failed to act as an efficient and dynamic financial intermediary (see Cole and Slade [1996] and McLeod [1994]). When the technocrats saw the window of liberalization open slightly, they immediately seized on the opportunity, and removed most significant regulatory barriers to entry, pricing, ownership and customer service. Suddenly, a predominantly private-owned and seemingly dynamic banking sector sprang to life. The range of financial services expanded dramatically, competition intensified, many more borrowers and lenders entered financial markets, and margins between deposit and lending rates were reduced. Foreign banks were permitted more liberalized entry, but the major players were domestic.

There is no doubt that this financial deregulation spurred faster economic development. But it was a high-risk strategy, owing mainly to the almost complete absence of follow-up prudential supervision. Financial statements were not reliable, banks lent to many high-risk projects without careful evaluation of the stakes, there was much inter-affiliate trading, "command lending" to powerful individuals and interests remained just as significant as before, there was an acute shortage of human resources, and perhaps most important Bank Indonesia was not able to keep up with the rapidly changing rules of the game.

In retrospect, one of the great tragedies in the recent history of Indonesian economic policy making is that, having introduced the financial liberalization, the technocrats were shortly afterwards disempowered significantly, with the result that the crucial checks and balances were never put in place. Even in countries with well-managed and regulated systems, financial deregulation has often been followed by spectacular collapses.[58] In Indonesia's case, the explosive cocktail was huge inflows of speculative and short-term capital, an increasingly politicized and corrupt business environment, poor financial reporting standards, and weak enforcement (Cole and Slade 1998).

The immediate issue in the crisis economies is the injection of new funds to recapitalize their financial institutions. The longer-term challenge is to put in place a regulatory framework which ensures that such crises are not repeated. This is a large issue beyond our immediate scope, but there is an emerging professional consensus concerning the policy reform agenda for the domestic financial sector in economies like Indonesia.[59] The overriding requirement is that financial institutions are trusted and credible. In this context, several points deserve emphasis:

- Capital adequacy ratios need to meet minimum (and conservative) specified prudential standards.
- Financial regulations need to be all-embracing, in the sense that any significant-sized entity needs to come under its jurisdiction. Obviously, this definition includes hedge funds; it probably excludes informal sector financial operations unless they are very sizeable.
- Financial data need to be of the highest quality, and to be widely reported to and disseminated among the investing public. This in turn requires the strictest disclosure requirements, the maintenance of international-standard technical auditing and accounting practices, and accurate information on the nature and extent of these institutions' non-performing loans.
- Financial institutions need to be encouraged to maintain a diversified asset portfolio, by sector and by country. There may be a case for limiting their exposure to one sector, particularly one — such as real estate — which is prone to boom and bust cycles.

- Practices such as related-party loans and insider trading obviously need to be prohibited.
- A set of legal institutions needs to be in place which severely punishes reckless "moral hazard" type behaviour which banks on official bail-outs for fear of a system-wide collapse, and which ensures that bankruptcy procedures work cleanly and expeditiously for creditors.
- There needs to be the highest quality regulatory authority, and one which is publicly accountable according to clearly specified performance criteria, whose decision-making processes are fully transparent, who are completely independent of political interference, and who are remunerated at levels which are competitive with those on offer in the activities which they oversee.

Whether Indonesia's newly emerging political system will have the capacity and the will to enact such a policy framework remains to be seen. The further the regulatory framework diverges from this first-best proposal, the weaker will be the argument for maintaining an open and liberal posture towards international capital flows, and for radical financial liberalization of the type introduced in 1988.

ENDNOTES

[1] The literature on these questions is expanding rapidly, and it is not possible to cite it comprehensively. Studies already published by early 1999, and featuring a special focus on Southeast Asia, include Jomo (ed, 1998), Lane et al. (1999), McLeod and Garnaut (1998), Montes (1998), Radelet and Sachs (1998), World Bank (1998*b*), and Arndt and Hill (1999). For Indonesia, McLeod (1998), Manning (1999), World Bank (1998*a*) and the 'Survey of Recent Developments' in *BIES* cover developments in more detail. Assessments by prominent Indonesian economists include Sadli (1999), Simandjuntak (1999) and Tubagus (1998). For the onset and early stages of the crisis, see in particular Soesastro and Basri (1998) and Johnson (1998).

[2] Of course, it is certainly the case that there exists a well established "gloom and despair industry", generally hostile to the notion of authoritarian, market-oriented, capitalist economies. The Indonesian variant of it had been forecasting the collapse of the Soeharto regime for a quarter of a century. But such a school of thought objected to these regimes largely on the grounds of abuse of human rights, limited political freedoms, and corruption, rather than providing a coherent analytical framework to explain why the economic development strategy might be unsustainable. For analyses of these approaches, by Japanese and US scholars, see respectively Yasuba (1994) and Emmerson (nd).

[3] For example, as the Bank data show, Indonesia's life expectancy was lower and its infant mortality rate was higher than China, the Philippines and Vietnam, all countries with similar or lower pre-crisis per capita GDP.

[4] In fairness to Krugman, it should be pointed out that the conclusions from his myth paper, if correct, pointed to a gradual slowing down of growth rates, not the catastrophic collapse in economic activity which has occurred since mid-1997, a point Krugman himself has made in commenting on the East Asian crisis.

[5] Ironically, Peregrine's owner was also an outspoken defender of authoritarian Asian regimes and the "Asian" way of doing business.

[6] Note that quarterly national accounts data are published regularly, but they are not yet considered particularly reliable. The quarterly production and expenditure data for 1998, for example, show implausibly large swings, much more than would be expected even allowing for seasonal agricultural fluctuations. As a corollary, it is therefore going to be difficult to pinpoint with any accuracy when the Indonesian economy has finally bottomed.

It is also needs to be emphasized that, in the context of recovery from a deep recession, the quarterly growth numbers are especially sensitive to the selection of the base period on which the growth numbers are calculated. For example, in the first quarter of 1999, the Indonesian economy either grew 1.3% (compared to the last quarter of 1998) or contracted 10% (compared to the same quarter in 1998).

[7] As this item is dominated by civil service wages, it reflects as much as anything trends in real public sector wages.

[8] Late January 1998 also marked the end of the fasting month, when liquidity traditionally rises.

[9] In the context of this general decline, however, the market does seem to have been quite discerning in its share write-downs, since companies with close ties to former president Soeharto and those which are import-intensive operations catering to the domestic market for consumer durables have been subject to particularly savage treatment. Examples of each include Bimantara (a conglomerate owned by Soeharto's second son, Bambang) and Astra (a major auto producer),

whose stock market valuations had declined by 95% and 85% respectively *in rupiah terms* over this period.

[10] If the figures are to be believed, the increase occurred in both urban and rural areas. Indeed, and perhaps indicative of the serious situation in the cities, urban agricultural employment is reported to have risen about 45%. This was equivalent to 29% of the increase in rural areas, even though pre-crisis 93% of the agricultural labour force was located in rural areas.

[11] Alternative indicators give something of the flavour of the beneficial effects of increased returns to cash crop agriculture. For example, in South Sulawesi, where much small-holder cocoa is produced, rural school enrolments rose markedly in 1998. It is also reported that motor vehicle registrations and *haj* pilgrimages increased.

[12] See Booth (1999), Cameron (1999) and Poppele et al. (1999) for discussion of data and methodological estimates associated with these estimates.

[13] In passing, one cannot help but note that the earlier, exaggerated poverty estimates, while no doubt motivated by a commendable concern for the poor during the crisis, may well have ended up doing much harm to the cause of the poor. This is so because the release of more careful poverty analysis, demonstrating that these estimates were very misleading, has introduced the very real risk that the government and the international donor community now feel under less pressure to maintain funding for a range of social safety net programs.

[14] For example, the data are at best suggestive in a number of respects: the primary school data are not age-specific (that is, allowing for the impact of falling fertility levels on this age group); the decline in junior secondary school enrolments had begun pre-crisis; large declines occurred in unexpected locations (e.g., urban Maluku, relatively unaffected by the crisis); and enrolment data for remote rural areas are some-what elastic.

[15] The IMF's *World Economic Outlook* (various issues) reports the

following annual average capital flows to emerging capital markets ($ billions):

	1977–82	1983–89	1990–94	1995	1996	1997
Total	30.5	8.8	120.8	192.0	240.8	173.7
Asia	15.8	16.7	40.1	95.8	110.4	13.9

[16] There is of course a long tradition of analyses of corruption and poor quality governance in Indonesia and elsewhere in the region (see, for example, Backman 1999 and Yoshihara 1988), but this literature does not necessarily draw the link between these weaknesses and economic/financial crises.

[17] It might be noted in passing that the World Bank played a relatively minor role over this period. This is presumably explained in part by the fact that the Fund has the major mandate for handling currency and financial crises. But one also has the impression that the Bank now operates under such a diverse and over-loaded mandate that its effectiveness in key economic policy areas has been diminished.

[18] See Ammar (1997), Bhanupong (1999) and Warr (1998) for careful analyses.

[19] Baig and Goldfajn (1998) test this proposition using daily financial (stock market and exchange rate) data, and careful analysis of major domestic news reporting and events. They found the evidence of contagion to be particularly pronounced in the foreign debt markets, but less so in stock markets. They conclude that "... after controlling for own country news and a few other fundamentals, the cross-country correlations in the currency and equity markets remain large and significant. ... The evidence of contagion in the foreign debt market reinforces the view that there was an element of financial panic at the onset of the Asian crisis". (p. 42)

[20] See Jotzo (1998) for a very detailed compilation and analysis of early warning and vulnerability indicators.

[21] This is not the place for an in-depth analysis of Indonesia's external debt statistics, other than to stress their obvious weaknesses, and the clear signal that Bank Indonesia's inadequacy sends to markets. Admittedly, an open capital account renders more difficult the task of collecting reliable

time series data. But BI's inability pre-crisis to estimate accurately total debt and its major components points to significant institutional failure. The problems clearly reside mainly in the private sector and short-term categories. The range of estimates of the latter is a particularly serious problem, as it is often considered to be a key vulnerability indicator.

Already, since the onset of the crisis, BI has "discovered" more than $10 billion of previously unrecorded debt and, as the auditing processes continue, further upward revisions can be expected. It should also be noted that the distinction between what constitutes "private" and "public" debt is often blurred, owing to various implicit and explicit government guarantees on private borrowings. Since many of these guarantees were conferred on Soeharto family enterprises, which now or are likely to be subject to legal action, it may be some time yet before the magnitudes can be accurately estimated.

[22] As World Bank (1998*b*, p. 8) shows, among the crisis economies Indonesia and Korea had the highest ratio of M2/international reserves, while Indonesia's short term debt to reserves ratio was second only to Korea.

[23] This is not to say that, at the micro-level, all government expenditures were sensible. Obviously they were not, but that is not necessarily a major consideration in judgements about the macroeconomic policy framework.

The other caveat to be attached to the fiscal policy record is that it is much easier to achieve good fiscal outcomes during a period of strong growth, and thus the more relevant indicator of fiscal policy is the "structural" or underlying deficit, rather than the "headline" figure being referred to here.

[24] Conversely, it would be naive to argue that hedging alone would have been a simple cure-all. First, financial markets were still at an embryonic stage, and were developing more slowly than the build-up of private debt. Secondly, the presence of hedging agents might simply have transferred the problem of flight out of rupiah from the borrowing firms to the financial

intermediaries. That is, the scramble for dollars in late 1997, in anticipation of a further declining rupiah, would have been instigated by the insurers rather than the borrowers. (This argument, however, ignores the role of internationally diversified insurance facilities, in which rupiah holdings would presumably be very small.)

[25] This is based in part on the argument that Indonesia's mix of vulnerability indicators (high debt/GDP but moderate domestic credit/GDP ratios) was such that a large exchange rate depreciation could do more damage than an interest rate increase. By contrast, the reverse argument is sometimes applied to Malaysia, given its lower debt but higher domestic credit ratios. See Goldfajn and Baig (1998), especially the indicators assembled on p. 26, for more on this.

[26] For example, Radelet and Sachs (1998) present a series of REERs based on wholesale price indices which show significant appreciations over the period 1990–96 in Indonesia, Malaysia, the Philippines and Thailand. Athukorala and Warr (1999) estimated tradable/non-tradable price ratios for Indonesia and Thailand over this period and found significant appreciations, especially in Thailand.

[27] As a percentage of commercial banks loans, Bank Indonesia reported these ratios as follows:

	1993	1994	1995	1996
NPLs	14.2	12.1	10.4	8.8
Bad loans	3.3	4.0	3.3	2.9

[28] For example, Bank Indonesia reported in 1995 that among the 240 state, private, foreign/joint venture and local development banks, some 21 were operating below the required capital adequacy ratio, 70 exceeded the legal lending limit, and 18 had excessive loan-deposit ratios. These data do not give any indication of by how far designated performance indicators were being missed, or the size of the banks involved; private and foreign/joint venture banks were more commonly involved than state or local development banks.

[29] See, for example, Cole and Slade (1996) and the contributors to McLeod (1994).

REFERENCES

(Note: *BIES* refers to the *Bulletin of Indonesian Economic Studies*.)

Ammar Siamwalla. 1997. *Thailand's Boom and Bust: Collected Papers.* Bangkok: Thailand Development Research Institute.

APEG (Asia Pacific Economics Group). 1998. *Asia Pacific Profiles 1998.* Canberra: Australian National University.

Arndt, H.W. 1944. *The Economic Lessons of the Nineteen Thirties.* Oxford: Oxford University Press.

Arndt, H.W. and H. Hill, eds. 1999. *Southeast Asia's Economic Crisis: Origins, Lessons, and the Way Forward.* Singapore: Institute of Southeast Asian Studies and Sydney: Allen & Unwin, New York: St Martin's Press.

Aswicahyono, H.H. 1998. "Total Factor Productivity in Indonesian Manufacturing, 1975–1993". Unpublished PhD thesis. Canberra: Australian National University.

Athukorala, P-C. and P. Warr. 1999. "Vulnerability to a Currency Crisis: Lessons from the East Asian Experience". Forthcoming Working Paper. Canberra: Australian National University.

Atinc, T.A. and M. Walton. 1998. "East Asia's Social Model after the Crisis". Unpublished Working Paper. Washington, D.C.: World Bank.

Backman, M. 1999. *Asian Eclipse: Exposing the Dark Side of Business in Asia.* Singapore: John Wiley & Sons.

Baig, T. and I. Goldfajn. 1998. "Financial Market Contagion in the Asian Crisis". IMF Working Paper 98/155. Washington, D.C.

Bardhan, P. 1997. "Corruption and Development: A Review of the Issues". *Journal of Economic Literature*, 35, pp. 1320–346.

Bhagwati, J. 1998. "The Capital Myth". *Foreign Affairs* 77, no. 7–12.

Bhanupong Nidhiprabha. 1999. "Economic Crisis and the Debt-Deflation Episode in Thailand". In Arndt and Hill, eds, pp. 67–80.

Bird, K. 1999. "Industrial Concentration and Competition in Indonesian Manufacturing". Unpublished PhD dissertation. Canberra: Australian National University.

Booth, A. 1999. "The Impact of the Crisis on Poverty and Equity". In Arndt and Hill, eds, pp. 128–41.

Browne, C. 1997. "Comment", on J. Soedradjad Djiwandono, "The Banking Sector in Emerging Markets: The Case of Indonesia". In *Banking Soundness and Monetary Policy: Issues and Experiences in the Global Economy*, ed. C. Enoch and J.H. Green. Washington, D.C.: IMF, pp. 349–52.

Cameron, L. 1999. "Survey of Recent Developments". *BIES* 35, no. 1.

Chen, E.K.Y. 1997. "The Total Factor Productivity Debate: Determinants of Economic Growth in East Asia". *Asian-Pacific Economic Literature* 11, no. 1: pp. 18–38.

Claessens S. et al. 1998. "Corporate Distress in East Asia: Assessing the Damage of Interest and Exchange Rate Shocks". Unpublished paper. World Bank, Washington, D.C.

Cole, D.C. and B.F. Slade. 1996. *Building a Modern Financial System: The Indonesian Experience.* Cambridge: Cambridge University Press.

Cole, D.C. and B.F. Slade. 1998. "Why has Indonesia's Financial Crisis been so bad?" *BIES* 34, no. 2: pp. 61–66.

Cole, D.C. and B.F. Slade. 1999. "The Crisis and Financial Sector Reform". In Arndt and Hill, eds, pp. 107–18.

Corbett, J. and D. Vines. 1998. "Asian Currency and Financial Crises: Lessons from Vulnerability, Crisis, and Collapse". *World Economy* 22, no. 3.

Corden, W. M. 1998. *The Asian Crisis: Is There a Way Out?* Singapore: Institute of Southeast Asian Studies.

Dornbusch, R., I. Goldfajn, R.O. Valdes. 1995. "Currency Crises and Collapses". Brookings Papers on Economic Activity 2, pp. 219–93.

	July 1997	September 1998	April 1999
Indonesia	118	1,667	784
Thailand	98	648	191
Malaysia	65	1,011	275
South Korea	na	689	213
China	78	249	161

[51] Lane et al. (1999, p. 91) highlight how different Indonesia has been in the financing of its fiscal deficit in its first programme year (i.e., under the IMF), 1998/99. Fully 84% of its deficit is estimated to have been foreign-financed, compared to 31% in Korea in 1998 and 11% in Thailand in 1997/98.

[52] For example, through to 31 March 1999, of the 50 petitions brought to court, only 13 have led to bankruptcies. The others have been suspended (11), rejected (10), settled (9) or pending (7). Few of the cases thus far brought to court have involved large companies.

[53] For example, Booth (1999) suggests that rice subsidies might be confined to low-grade varieties.

[54] There have been three main forms of controls (see Laban and Larrain [1998], as cited in the *Economist*, 14 March 1998, for more details): (a) 30% of all non-equity capital entering the country must be deposited without interest at the central bank for one year; (b) Chilean firms and banks can tap international capital markets only if two ratings agencies rate their paper as high as Chilean government bonds; and (c) foreign money must stay in the country for at least a year.

It is worth noting that in mid-1998 the 30% regulation was reduced to 10% in the wake of fears that, as the Chilean peso fell, the requirement was discouraging capital inflow.

[55] Conversely, however, it should be noted that the efficacy of the Chilean approach is a matter of some controversy in the literature. Some country experts (e.g., Edwards 1998*b*) have argued that they were not central to the country's success, and were much less important than the financial reforms.

[56] One is reminded once again of the observations over a decade ago of one of Indonesia's most influential economists:

In 1954/5, I was a strong protagonist of foreign exchange controls. I felt that we only had the state to fight against the "big five". Then I saw what happened under Ali Sastro and Soekarno. In 1983 there was a movement towards the reimposition of foreign exchange controls. I went to the President and argued strongly against it. I know how easy it is to smuggle goods and I know that those who are close to the sources of power will get their hands on the foreign exchange. (Sumitro Djojohadikusumo 1986, pp. 38–39.)

[57] That is, for example, a significant decline in the country's terms of trade would have to be matched by falling domestic costs — including wages — to restore international competitiveness. Such an issue has confronted Argentina during the current period of weak commodity prices, and it may have pushed the country further into recession that would otherwise have been the case. Conversely, it might still be argued that this was a price worth paying for long-term monetary stability.

[58] In practice, as Grenville (1998, p. 21) observes, the ideal of financial deregulation being accompanied by comprehensive and effective supervision is everywhere extremely difficult to realize: "It is difficult — perhaps impossible — to put in place fully effective supervision *before* financial development occurs: the markets will be pushing ahead faster than supervisors."

[59] See Cole and Slade (1999), Fane (1998), and Johnston (1998).

surprisingly— has reached such a conclusion. See Lane et al. (1999) and Goldfajn and Baig (1998).

In assessing Indonesian monetary policy during the worst months of the crisis, it needs to be emphasized again that, as noted above in the context of Figure 3, Indonesia's loose monetary policy was not so much the result of a deliberate strategy of reflation as several episodes of panic (and probable acquiescence to political pressures) on the part of the central bank in response to some major bank runs which occurred from late 1997.

[43] Japan is Indonesia's largest commercial creditor by a large margin. According to Bank for International Settlements data, as at 30 June 1998, Japanese creditors account for 38% of this debt; the next largest creditor is Germany, with 12%. There seems little doubt that the reluctance of Japanese financial institutions to accept write-downs, owing to their own parlous circumstances, has complicated and delayed the debt re-solution process.

[44] By early 1999 this problem had become much less serious, in part because of good rice crops. But an FAO/WFP memo of April 1999 ("Crop and Food Supply Assessment Mission to Indonesia", Rome) noted that traders were still tending to hold below normal stock levels.

[45] The key document in this context is the report of the "Canberra Conference", involving a group of senior econo-mists from Indonesia, Australia, Japan and the USA, and held at the Australian National University, 23–25 November 1998. Its "Report of a Conference on Indonesia's Economic Crisis" was published bilingually in January 1999 by the Fakultas Ekonomi, Universitas Indonesia. See in particular Manning (1999), who presents the Report and places it in a broader analytical and political economy context.

[46] The one obvious caveat to this conclusion, noted above, is that its banks, which on a country basis have by far the largest stake in Indonesia, appear thus far reluctant to accept write-downs on their outstanding debts. The contrast here with the US is noticeable: it is now a very minor aid donor to Indonesia,

but its financial institutions do appear more willing to do deals in the process of seeking a resolution of their debt problems.

[47] Already there are beginnings of initiatives in this direction. In late April, Parliament passed a bill specifying revenue sharing arrangements for resource-rich provinces. Under the new arrangements, provinces will be permitted to retain 15%, 30%, and 80% of the revenue obtained from oil, gas, and forestry and fisheries respectively. But much more is likely to follow in terms of sweeping administrative and budgetary measures.

[48] Indonesia's new politicians would also endorse strongly the remarks in June 1998 of the then Malaysian Deputy Prime Minister, Anwar Ibrahim, who has close ties with many of them:

> "It is as if the crisis unleashed a gale of creative destruction that will cleanse society of collusion, cronyism and nepotism. … The result will be a leaner and revitalized market economy, based on fairness and competition on a level playing field, where big corporations, small businesses and all citizens have equal access to capital and resources." (*Far Eastern Economic Review*, 18 July 1998, p. 11.)

[49] Indonesia might do well to follow Dornbusch's (1997, p. 22) injunction that "[g]ood macroeconomic management leaves a bit of room on every front and offers plenty of transparency." In particular, it avoids "drawing hard lines in the sand" on exchange rates, gambling foreign reserves away and getting a maximum of foreign capital on very short maturity, while also maintaining room for interest rates to be raised if necessary.

[50] Trends in the latter are, however, quite encouraging. Indonesia was perceived as by far the most risky investment through 1998, and it is still very much an outlier compared with the other crisis economies. But the risk premium has fallen considerably, as indicated by Asian bond spreads over US Treasury Bonds (in basis points):

[30] See Jotzo (1998), Lane et al. (1999), and World Bank (1998*b*).

[31] See Bardhan (1997) for a survey and analysis of the corruption literature, including various ranking exercises.

[32] If the *Time* report is to be believed, natural resource based activities dominated the family's revenue stream over the 30-year period of power, with oil and gas (23% of the total), forestry and plantations (14%), petrochemicals (9%) and mining (8%) constituting over half the revenue. Apart from interest on deposits (12%), no other sector contributed more than 7% of the total.

[33] For the record, it is worth remembering that when the state oil company, Pertamina, crashed in 1975 owing to blatant mismanagement, its debts were approximately equivalent to 30% of GDP (McCawley 1978).

[34] In the words of the Malaysian Prime Minister, Mahathir Mohamad:
> "So many of the ... main causes of the financial and currency turmoil — corruption, monopoly, crony capitalism ... – have always been with us. Yet we were able to grow faster and longer than anyone before in human history." (*Far Eastern Economic Review*, 18 July 1998, p. 19.)

[35] As Lane et al. (1999, p. 108) observe: "In addition to the limited coverage for deposits in private banks, the guarantee was not widely publicized, and no announcement was made regarding the treatment of depositors in other institutions that had not yet been intervened."

[36] Notable among these, for example, were the presidential family's banking and infrastructure interests. Bambang Trihatmodjo's Bank Andromeda had been closed as part of the 1 November 1997 package, but he quickly re-entered the industry via another bank, Bank Alfa. Some of the family's infrastructure projects which had been frozen as part of the fiscal austerity measures were also re-activated.

[37] In advancing this argument, however, one has to be mindful of the counter-argument, that the centralization of corruption may confer greater predictability in the system. Observing that corruption assessments generally rank India and

Indonesia similarly, Bardhan (1997, p. 1325) conjectures that Indonesia's superior economic performance in these circumstances may have been due to India's 'more fragmented, often anarchic, system of bribery'.

[38] On the Philippine crisis in the mid 1980s, see May and Nemenzo (eds, 1985), and Vos and Yap (1996).

[39] Some might counter this "historical accident" thesis with the argument that the weakening of the technocrats' influence in the cabinet was a deliberate strategy of the Soeharto family. Such a thesis holds up well for the last, short-lived Soeharto cabinet of March 1998. There is no doubt also that, during the 1990s, several top Finance and Bank Indonesia officials, who had began their careers in 'technocratic' moulds, had been progressively drawn into the Soeharto family orbit. (One prominent example (pointed out by Backman 1999, p. 287) was Dr Fuad Bawazier, the two-month Finance Minister in the March cabinet, and formerly Director General of Taxation, who was also chairman of son Bambang's telecommunication company, Satelindo.)

But one cannot also ignore the fact that the 1990s coincided with the passing of all the key "Berkeley Mafia", who had so ably guided Indonesian economic policy-making since the late 1960s, and whose members had an unparalleled capacity for influence over Soeharto (despite, oddly, the extremely limited recognition they received in the latter's autobiography — see Soeharto, 1989). The counter-factual thesis that, had they still been in positions of influence during the 1990s, they would have been able to curb the excesses of the regime, will always remain unverifiable.

[40] See for example Browne (1997), commenting on a paper delivered by Indonesia's central bank governor in January 1997.

[41] This is the argument commonly associated with Jeffrey Sachs of Harvard, that the IMF has appeared more intent on disciplining governments rather than on reassuring markets. See also Radelet and Sachs (1998) and Feldstein (1998).

[42] Recent IMF technical research plausibly — but perhaps not

INDEX

Soesastro, H. and M.C. Basri. 1998. "Survey of Recent Developments". *BIES* 34, no. 1.

Soros, G. 1998. "Towards a Global Open Society". *Atlantic Monthly* 281, no. 1: 20–32.

Sumitro Djojohadikusumo. 1986. "Recollections of my Career". *BIES* 22, no. 3: 27–39.

Timmer, M. 1999. "Indonesia's Ascent on the Technology Ladder: Capital Stock and Total Factor Productivity Levels in Indonesian Manufacturing, 1975–1995". *BIES* 35, no. 1: 75–97.

Tubagus Feridhanusetyawan. 1997. "Survey of Recent Developments". *BIES* 33, no. 2: 3–39.

Tubagus Feridhanusetyawan. 1998. "Social Impacts of the Indonesian Crisis". *Indonesian Quarterly* 26, no. 4: 325–64.

Vos, R. and J.T. Yap. 1996. *The Philippine Economy: East Asia's Stray Cat?* London: MacMillan.

Wanandi, S. 1999. "The Post-Soeharto Business Environment". In Forrester, ed, pp. 128–34.

Warr, P. 1998. "Thailand". In McLeod and Garnaut, eds, pp. 49–65.

de Wit, Y.B. 1973. "The Kabupaten Program". *BIES* 9, no. 1: 65–85.

World Bank. 1998*a*. *Indonesia in Crisis: A Macroeconomic Update.* Washington, D.C.

World Bank. 1998*b*. *East Asia: The Road to Recovery,* Washington, D.C.

Yasuba, Y. 1994. "The Economic History of Southeast Asia through Japanese Glasses, 1970–90". Paper presented to the Annual Meeting of the Economic History Association, October.

Yoshihara K. 1988. *The Rise of Ersatz Capitalism in Southeast Asia.* Singapore: Oxford University Press.

MacIntyre, A. 1999. "Political Institutions and the Economic Crisis in Thailand and Indonesia". In Arndt and Hill, eds, pp. 142–57.

McKibbin, W. 1999. "Modelling the Crisis in Asia". In Arndt and Hill, eds, pp. 119–27.

Mackie, J. 1998. "Soothing Indonesia's Resentments". *Asian Wall Street Journal*, 10 September.

Mackie, J.A.C. and A. MacIntyre. 1994. "Politics". In *Indonesia's New Order: The Dynamics of Socio-Economic Transformation* ed. H. Hill, pp. 1–53. Sydney: Allen & Unwin, pp. 1–53.

McKinnon, R.I. 1993. *The Order of Economic Liberalization: Financial Control in the Transition to a Market Economy*. Baltimore: Johns Hopkins University Press.

McKinnon, R.I. and H. Pill. 1998. "International Overborrowing: A Decomposition of Credit and Currency Risks". *World Development* 26, no. 7: 1267–282.

McLeod, R. ed. 1994. *Indonesia Assessment 1994: Finance as a Key Sector in Indonesia's Development*. Singapore: Institute of Southeast Asian Studies.

McLeod, R. 1997. "Explaining Chronic Inflation in Indonesia". *Journal of Development Studies*, 33, no. 2: 392–410.

McLeod, R. 1998. "Indonesia". In McLeod and Garnaut, eds, pp. 31–48.

McLeod, R. and R. Garnaut, eds. 1998. *East Asia in Crisis: From Being a Miracle to Needing One?* London: Routledge.

Manning, C. 1998. *Indonesian Labour in Transition: An East Asian Success Story?* Cambridge: Cambridge University Press.

Manning, C. 1999. "Indonesia's Economic Collapse and Path to Recovery: Can (and Should) the Leopard Change its Spots?" Development Studies Papers. Canberra: Asia-Pacific School of Economics and Management, Australian National University.

Martinez, G.O. 1998. "What Lessons Does the Mexican Crisis Hold for Recovery in Asia?' *Finance and Development* 35, no. 2: 6–9.

May, R.J. and F. Nemenzo, eds. 1985. *The Philippines after Marcos*. London: Croom Helm.

MOEC/World Bank. 1999. *The Impact of Indonesia's Economic Crisis on Education: Findings from a Survey of Schools.* Jakarta: Office of Research and Development, Ministry of Education and Culture.

Montes, M.F. 1998. *The Currency Crisis in Southeast Asia.* Singapore: Institute of Southeast Asian Studies.

Montgomery, J. 1997. "The Indonesian Financial System: Its Contribution to Economic Performance, and Policy Issues". IMF Working Paper 97/45, Washington, D.C.

OECD (Organization for Economic Cooperation and Development) (1998), *OECD Economic Surveys 1997–98: Mexico,* Paris.

Poppele, J., Sudarno Sumarto and L. Pritchett. 1999. "Social Impacts of the Indonesian Crisis: New Data and Policy Implications". Unpublished paper. Jakarta: SMERU (Social Monitoring and Early Response Unit).

Radelet, S. and J. Sachs. 1998. "The East Asian Financial Crisis: Diagnosis, Remedies, Prospects". *Brookings Papers on Economic Activity,* pp. 1–90.

Radius Prawiro. 1998. *Indonesia's Struggle for Economic Development: Pragmatism in Action.* Kuala Lumpur: Oxford University Press.

Sadli, M. 1999. "The Indonesian Crisis". In Arndt and Hill, eds, pp. 16–27.

Sandee, H. and Roos Kities Andadari. 1998. "The Impact of Indonesia's Financial Crisis on Clustered Enterprise: A Case Study of the Jepara Furniture Cluster". Unpublished paper.

Schwarz, A. 1994. *A Nation in Waiting: Indonesia in the 1990s.* Sydney: Allen & Unwin.

Simandjuntak, D.S. 1999. "An Inquiry into the Nature, Causes and Consequences of the Indonesian Crisis". *Journal of Asia-Pacific Economy* 4, no. 1: 171–92.

J. Soedradjad Djiwandono. 1999. "The Rupiah — One Year after its Float". In Forrester, ed, pp. 145–53.

Soeharto. 1989. *Pikiran, Ucapan, dan Pikiran Saya: Otobiografi* [My Thoughts, Sayings, and Actions: An Autobiography], as related to G. Dwipayana and K.H. Ramadhan. Jakarta: PT Cipta Lamtoro Gung Persada.

Dornbusch, R. 1997. "A Thai-Mexico Primer". *The International Economy*, September/October, pp. 20–23.

Edwards, S. 1998*a*. "The Mexican Peso Crisis: How Much did we know? When did we know it?" *World Economy* 21, no. 1: pp. 1–30.

Edwards, S. 1998*b*. "Asia Should beware of Chilean-style Capital Controls". *Asian Wall Street Journal*, 8 April 1998.

Emmerson, D. nd. "The Rabbit and the Crocodile: Expecting the End of the New Order in Indonesia, 1966–91". Unpublished paper. University of Wisconsin, Madison.

Fane, G. 1998. "The Role of Prudential Regulation". In McLeod and Garnaut, eds, pp. 287–303.

Fane, G. and T. Condon. 1996. "Trade Reform in Indonesia, 1987–1995". *BIES*, 32, no. 3: 33–54.

Feldstein, M. 1998. "Refocusing the IMF". *Foreign Affairs* 77, no. 2: 20–33.

Forrester, G., ed. 1999. *Post-Soeharto Indonesia: Renewal or Chaos?* Singapore: Institute of Southeast Asian Studies.

Forrester, G. and R. May, eds. 1998. *The Fall of Soeharto.* Bathurst: Crawfurd Press.

Garnaut, R. 1998. "The Financial Crisis: A Watershed in Economic Thought about East Asia". *Asian-Pacific Economic Literature* 12, no. 1: 1–11.

Garnaut, R. 1999. "Exchange Rates in the East Asian Crisis", In Arndt and Hill, eds, pp. 93–106.

Goldfajn, I. and T. Baig. 1998. "Monetary Policy in the Aftermath of Currency Crises: The Case of Asia". IMF Working Paper 98/170. Washington, D.C.

Grenville, S. 1998. "Capital Flows and Crises". Unpublished paper. Sydney: Reserve Bank of Australia.

Hardy, D.C. and C. Pazarbasioglu 1998. "Leading Indicators of Banking Crises: Was Asia Different?" IMF Working Paper 98/91. Washington, D.C.

Hughes, H. 1999. "Corporatist (Crony) Capitalism and the East Asian 'Crisis'". Unpublished paper. Canberra: Australian National University.

ILO (International Labour Organization. 1998. *Employment Challenges of the Indonesian Economic Crisis.* Jakarta.

Jellinek, L. and Bambang Rustanto 1999. "Survival Strategies of the Javanese during the Economic Crisis". Uunpublished paper. Jakarta.

Johnson, C. 1998. "Survey of Recent Developments". *BIES*, 34, no. 2: 3–60.

Johnston, R.B. 1998. "Sequencing Capital Account Liberalizations and Financial Sector Reform". IMF Papers on Policy Analysis and Assessment 98/8. Washington, D.C.

Jomo K.S., ed. 1998. *Tigers in Trouble: Financial Crises, Liberalisation and Crises in East Asia.* London: Zed Books.

Jotzo, F. 1998. "The East Asian Currency Crises: Lessons for an Early Warning System". Economics Division Working Paper, APSEM/RSPAS. Australian National University.

Kenward, L.R. 1999. "Indonesia's Property Sector and the Economic Crisis of 1997/98". World Bank. Unpublished paper. Washington, D.C.: World Bank.

Kindleberger, C.P. 1989. *Manias, Panics and Crashes: A History of Financial Crises.* New York: Basic Books.

Krugman, P. 1979. "A Model of Balance of Payments Crises". *Journal of Money, Credit and Banking* 11, pp. 311–25.

Krugman, P. 1994. "The Myth of Asia's Miracle". *Foreign Affairs* 73, no. 6: pp. 62–78.

Krugman, P. 1997. "Latin Lessons for Asia". *Far Eastern Economic Review,* 25 October 1999.

Laban, R. and F. Larrain. 1998. "The Return of Private Capital to Chile in the 1990s: Causes, Effects, and Policy Reactions". Faculty Research Working Paper R98-02, John F. Kennedy School of Government, Harvard University.

Lane, T. et al. 1999. "IMF-Supported Programs in Indonesia, Korea and Thailand: A Preliminary Assessment". Washington, D.C., International Monetary Fund.

Lindsey, T. 1998. "The IMF and Insolvency Law Reform in Indonesia', *BIES*, 34, no. 3: 119–24.

McCawley, P. 1978. "Some Consequences of the Pertamina Crisis in Indonesia', *Journal of Southeast Asian Studies*, 9, no. 1: pp. 1–27.

THE AUTHOR

HAL HILL is Professor of Economics and Heaad of the Southeast Asia Economy Program in the Research School of Pacific and Asian Studies and the Asia-Pacific School of Economics and Management, Australian National University. From 1986 to 1998 he headed the University's Indonesia Project and for much of this time also edited the *Bulletin of Indonesian Economic Studies.*

His main research interests are the economies of ASEAN, especially Indonesia; industrialization and foreign investment in East Asia; and Australia's economic relations with the Asia-Pacific region.

His many books include *Foreign Investment and Industrialization in Indonesia* (1988), *Indonesia's New Order: The Dynamics of Socio-Economic Transformation* (1994) and *Southeast Asia's Economic Crisis* (1999).

He has worked as a consultant for the Australian Government, the Indonesian Government, the World Bank, the Asian Development Bank, and several United Nations agencies. He has held visiting appointments at Gadjah Mada University, University of the Philippines, Institute of Southeast Asian Studies, University of Oxford, Columbia University, and Thammasat University. He is also on the editorial board of nine academic journals.